Ref
LB
1775.4
.G7
B08
2000

D1468250

TEACHERS AND THE STATE

In the context of a fierce contemporary debate about attempts to 'modernise' the teaching profession, this book examines the status, training and continuing professional development of teachers on a national and international level. Based upon original research, the argument is developed that global competition is powerfully reshaping national approaches to professionalisation. The authors adopt the challenging position that teaching is being *de*professionalised through an increasing lack of autonomy, whilst being *re*professionalised as a result of the legislated use of esoteric structures and methods which exclude those not inducted in these approaches.

From this investigation comes a powerful verdict: contemporary re-professionalisation is insufficient, and the new agendas are preventing the kind of adaptability and reflective practice essential for the empowerment of pupils, parents and local communities.

In its synthesis of empirical research and recommendations for action, *Teachers and the State* makes essential reading for anybody with an interest in educational policy-making, teaching or professionalism.

Mike Bottery is Reader in Education, and Head of the Centre for Educational Studies, at the University of Hull. He has written widely in the field of teaching and education, and has taught in the UK, Europe, North America and the Far East.

Nigel Wright is Lecturer in Education at the University of Hull, was formerly Director of the Secondary PGCE, and is now Director for the PhD in Education programme in Hong Kong.

ROUTLEDGE RESEARCH IN EDUCATION

BELL LIBRARY-TAMU-CC

TEACHERS AND THE STATE

Towards a directed profession

Mike Bottery and Nigel Wright

London and New York

First published 2000
by Routledge
11 New Fetter Lane, London EC4P 4EE

Simultaneously published in the USA and Canada
by Routledge
29 West 35th Street, New York, NY 10001

Routledge is an imprint of the Taylor & Francis Group

© 2000 Mike Bottery and Nigel Wright

Typeset in Sabon by
MHL Typesetting Limited, Coventry
Printed and bound in Great Britain by
MPG Books Ltd, Bodmin

All rights reserved. No part of this book may be reprinted or reproduced
or utilised in any form or by any electronic, mechanical, or other means,
now known or hereafter invented, including photocopying and recording,
or in any information storage or retrieval system, without permission in
writing from the publishers.

British Library Cataloguing in Publication Data
A catalogue record for this book is available
from the British Library

Library of Congress Cataloging in Publication Data
Bottery, Mike.
  Teachers and the state: towards a directed profession / Mike Bottery
  and Nigel Wright
    p.   cm.
  Includes bibliographical references (p.) and index.
  1. Teachers–Great Britain.   2. Education and state–Great Britain.
  3. Teachers–Training of–Great Britain.   4. Teachers–Cross cultural
  studies.   I. Wright, Nigel.   II. Title.

I.B1775.41.G7 B68 2000
371.P00941   dc21   99-053301

ISBN 0-415-21347-9

CONTENTS

FIGURES

TABLES

ACKNOWLEDGEMENTS

We would like to thank all those teachers who took the time to reply to our questionnaires. We would also like to express special thanks to two of our colleagues: to Jeff Moore for advice on some of the trickier aspects of developing questionnaires; and to Derek Webster for doing the necessary, and valuable job of proof reading and commenting on the manuscript.

The authors are grateful to the following for permission to reproduce published material covered by copyright.

Carfax Publishing Limited, PO Box 25, Abingdon, Oxon, OX14 3UE; for material from *Journal of Education for Teaching*, 'Perceptions of Professionalism by the Mentors of Student Teachers' 23, 3: 1997, and

Teachers and Teaching, 'Teacher Professionalisation Through Action Research – possibility or pipe-dream?' 3, 2: 1997.

Sage Publications for material from *Educational Management and Administration*, 25, 1: 'Impoverishing a Sense of Professionalism: Who's to Blame?'

Blackwell Publishers for *British Journal of Educational Studies* 44, 1: 'Co-operating in their own Deprofessionalisation? On the need to recognise the "public" and "ecological" roles of the teaching profession'.

INTRODUCTION

This book describes the evidence of research findings which began in early 1992 and continued into 1999. The results of that research are very simply stated: they indicate that government priorities in the UK have meshed with a professional culture of teaching to produce a damaging coherence, one that has resulted in a weakening of an extended notion of the role of the professional, has reduced the influence of a key profession in the development of a thriving civil society, and at the same time has probably weakened the potentiality for a genuine political democracy.

The book, however, goes beyond these research findings. Whilst it examines the status, training and continuing professional development of teachers in England and Wales, it also examines the situation of teachers in other countries. It suggests that whilst there are differences between these situations, the similarities are more profound, and that the evidence suggests that the profession of teaching is being changed on an international scale, both in terms of its role and impact, and invariably for the worse.

The research we present from the UK is of relevance to the larger picture, we believe, because much of this change at an international level has been encapsulated in what has happened in education over the last 20 years in the UK. Such change has occurred along a spectrum from market led to government controlled. Under Margaret Thatcher, the direction in education was largely towards a more market-led approach, through such legislation as that to do with the devolution of finance to schools, enhanced opportunities for parents to enrol children at the school of their choice, the creation of a greater variety of schools, and greater provision of information in the form of examination results and inspection reports for 'parental consumers' to aid them in their selection of schools. Somewhat paradoxically this legislation was accompanied by the creation of a centralist National Curriculum, and was also undergirded by the belief that changes to a market-based consciousness could be accomplished initially only by a much more directive and dominant state (Gamble 1988). As the transition in power has been made from Thatcher, to Major, and then on to Blair, there has been a movement towards a more government-inspired and controlled agenda, the reasons for which will be

1

explained shortly. Markets, however, have not disappeared, but have become more managed, more subservient to central dictates. Whilst then there has been a process of movement along this spectrum, we suggest that the effect upon teachers and the teaching profession has, nevertheless, been much the same.

The teaching profession, we suggest, is being deprofessionalised through its increasing lack of autonomy in how and what it teaches. Whether the pressure comes from above (in terms of government direction) or from below (in terms of market forces), teachers no longer have the same degree of discretion they formerly had in what they teach and how they teach it. In England and Wales, for instance, there is now a very clear central agenda, where outcomes are specified, accompanied by detailed prescriptive regulations. But elsewhere, as indicated by writers like Caldwell and Spinks (1998), in the US, Canada, Australia, and New Zealand, the same movement to an outcomes-based approach, set within carefully specified criteria, is very much the order of the day. Further, if one were to think that a more market-based approach would produce greater flexibility and autonomy for teachers, the influence of markets must increasingly be understood within what might be called a post-Fordist approach to the management of public institutions. This is one where the control of policy and power is retained at the centre, and where the delegation of responsibility to the periphery is accompanied by a competitive framework in which providers are pitted against one another, and in which 'consumers' are provided with a variety of information by which their choices may be informed. There may then be autonomy in terms of some areas of implementation, but increasingly less in terms of why or what. In England and Wales, with the advent of the literacy and numeracy hours in primary schools, this increasingly includes how.

To recapitulate, since the high-water mark of Thatcherite and Reaganite free-marketisation, there has been a shift in governmental strategy worldwide along a spectrum which moves from market led to government directed. Whilst there is little doubt that movement generally is towards a more government-directed approach, there is quite heated debate concerning where governments and educational policies are on this spectrum. Phrases like 'New Deal', 'New Modernisers', and the 'Third Way', are all invoked to suggest a change of direction which in reality is still very much in the melting pot. Such terms are at bottom little more than a recognition that neither 'communism' (state dominance of societal activities), nor full-blown marketisation are any longer realistic policy possibilities for national governments, even if global debate on free markets still lags some way behind. Rather, the quest at national level is, within an overriding recognition that capitalism is the only viable form of economic order for the foreseeable future, to find an appropriate balance between the two. In such a situation, a 'Third Way' can – and does – involve all sorts of permutations, from education being located strongly on the 'state control' side of a Third Way continuum (as in the UK), to one where it is allowed to develop within a more market-oriented approach – even if a more managed one.

Wherever on a spectrum from 'market led' to 'government directed' a particular government takes a stand, however, the result appears to be the same – one in which governments control and direct the activities of the teaching profession, and in which the teaching profession apparently acquiesces. In order to appreciate the full implications of this situation, one needs to move beyond examining just this one spectrum of concern, that of market and state. One needs also to appreciate that the situation will be profoundly affected by the stance that a teaching profession takes, because the degree of its willingness to conform to government requirements will strongly affect the character of an education system, as well as the impact of that educational system on society at large.

A second spectrum may then be conceived as one that will then provide a scale of acquiescence which has at one end professionals of limited technical rationality, and at the other professionals who are more ecologically oriented. The first kind of professionals would believe that their job can be encapsulated by teaching a subject, handling the problems of children, and conforming to predetermined external dictates. At the other end of this spectrum ecological professionals would be those who believe that they must understand that to do their job effectively it is insufficient to deal just with classroom and institutional matters. Because so much of what affects schools and teachers lies within the wider society, it would then be felt incumbent to understand this ecology of forces acting upon the teaching profession, and upon schools, and to provide understandings, to both pupils and stakeholders, on the nature and effect of these forces. The two spectra thus described are combined and produced in Figure I.1

The result of combining state approaches with teachers' perceptions of their role leads to four very different kinds of schools, four very different types of education systems, and ultimately four very different kinds of society.

Combining a technical rational profession with a market-led approach would therefore lead to a teaching profession that saw its principal focus at the level of the institution, where notions of 'public good' were neglected in favour of the school's competitive advantage. Its criteria of success would be in terms of how many children it could recruit to its roll, the level of consumer satisfaction produced, and whether it managed to employ as many or more teachers than it did last year. This kind of result can be seen in research published by one of the authors of this book (Bottery 1998).

Combining a technical rational profession with government-directed policies would lead to the creation of a teaching profession that saw its principal focus as that of finding the right strategies, schedules, and procedures most efficiently to meet targets set externally, to respond most effectively to accountability criteria, and to implement most expediently central government directives. Its criteria of success would be whether it met

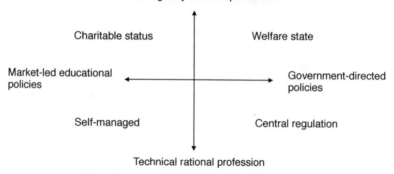

Figure 1.1 Combining state approaches to the teaching profession with teachers' perceptions of their own role.

the targets set externally, and whether it received favourable reports on its performance from the centre. Considerable elements of this approach are seen in the research reported in this book.

This book will argue that both of these combinations re-define what professionalism might mean. In the first case, professionalism would continue to include a belief in having specialised skills, as well as an altruistic belief in the purpose of teaching, but it would be re-defined by including within its definition what the individual can do to maximise the competitive advantage of his or her institution. In the second, this subject specialism would be re-defined to be those skills and knowledge that government thought was necessary for the carrying out of the teaching task, as well as the ability to meet external demands effectively and efficiently. These, it seems to us, are not simple cases of re-definition. Both moves reduce the strength of the term, and therefore not only reprofessionalise teachers but deprofessionalise them as well. This happens, then, because of the combination of particular government approaches towards education, and the prevailing professional culture. With different variables from either spectrum, neither of these situations would occur.

Therefore, the combination of a market-led policy with a more ecologically oriented profession would be likely to produce a situation in which the teaching profession, faced by a government that left matters of substantive public good to the determination of the market, would be likely to found private schools, preferably funded on a charitable basis, though as likely on a purely fee-paying basis. They would be like many existing independent schools which have been founded in the belief that specific ideals can be realised only outside the state sector. Their criterion of success would be, pragmatically, to survive in a market situation, but they would also have higher criteria. These would include the school's ability to transmit its values to its pupils, and for these to then have an impact upon the society within which the school was functioning. For those of an ecological orientation, such a market situation would not be ideal, but would allow an existence for their ideals.

The combination of more government-directed policies with a more ecologically oriented profession would probably create a situation not too unlike that of the welfare state in the UK in the 1940s–1960s – a system based upon the notion of altruistic and knowledgeable professionals contributing to the running of the educational system, though this time with a rather greater degree of conflict between professionals and central government than was seen previously. Such teachers' success criteria would be seen not only in their professional satisfaction at equipping their pupils for future roles in life, but would also transcend the concerns of a particular classroom or school, and would be used to contribute to the course of government policy and to produce a sense of public good, and the creation of a stable and harmonious society.

This book, however, is not arguing for any of the four positions described above. Instead, it will suggest that an appropriate combination of state approaches with teachers' perceptions lies in a relatively small area on the upper half of the teachers' perceptions of their role, and mid-way along the state approaches spectrum (Figure I.2). By placing our preferred combination in this area, we argue that neither a heavily market-oriented, nor a heavily state-directed approach to education is healthy. By striking a balance in the middle we suggest that it may be possible to take the best of both: a commitment to variety, experimentation, and ingenuity from market influences, and a commitment to public good and a stable civil society from state influences. But in itself, such a balance is insufficient. It needs to be enriched by a teaching profession that is aware of and willing to contribute towards the development of such a public good and such a civil society, and

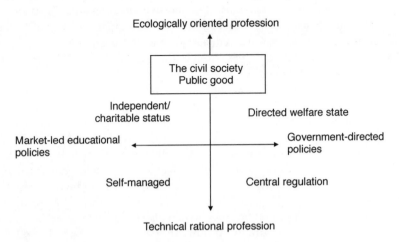

Figure I.2 Location of the public good.

which has the ingenuity and flair to do so. Only by such a combination can a satisfactory educational culture be created.

The first chapter, then, will begin by setting the context of teacher professionalism, by locating a review of educational policies and legislation in the UK and other selected countries within an overview of current global economic imperatives. This will be done in order to show how comparable economic concerns are impelling governments down similar roads in terms not only of education but policy in general, ones that retain strong policy direction from the centre, and which increasingly move away from market-driven approaches. A critique of what we shall call the 'New Moderniser' approach, based largely upon a participative model of citizenship education through an expanded conception of empowering professionalism located within an enhanced civil society, will be introduced here.

1

THE CONTEXT OF TEACHERS' DEPROFESSIONALISATION

Introduction: the historical context

The role and function of an education system, and of the teachers within it, have not recently and suddenly become matters of pressing political concern. Deliberation on such issues has been accompanied – indeed has largely prompted – the formation of systems since national systems were first conceived. The key word here, indeed, is 'national', because it was the creation of the nation-state that largely explains the development of the education systems we know today. Thus, the majority of the older education systems around the world – such as those in Germany, France, Italy, the United States, and Japan – were initially conceived at a time when these countries were pre-eminently concerned with questions of state formation. This was for a number of reasons: they might still be in the process of formation, in which ties were as at least as much to the local as to the national (France, Germany, United States); they might just have gone through a revolutionary period which called into question old assumptions, and/or were still seeking a legitimacy for their rule (France, Italy); or, finally, they might have gone through a period of foreign military and cultural invasion, and needed to establish their own cultural and political legitimacy (Germany, Japan, Italy). Their primary functions then were not initially driven by concerns for social equality, of a desire to spread a love of learning, or even with the advancement of economic performance by providing a workforce with the requisite skills and attitudes to service the industries of the countries involved. Instead, as Green (1997, p. 35) argues, they were designed

> ... to spread the dominant cultures and inculcate popular ideologies of nationhood, to forge the political and cultural unity of the burgeoning nation-states, and to cement the ideological hegemony of their dominant classes.

England is the example that proves the rule. It was a country with a greater political stability and fixed cultural identity than most, and it was the first

7

country to industrialise, and this before any serious conception of an educational system. In such circumstances, it is understandable that of the Western European countries, England was the slowest to develop a national system – there was, it was believed, less need. Only questions of social stability (making sure that a working class knew its place), of ethics (a belief by some of the right of all to an education) and of a dawning realisation of the need to be economically competitive, forced the late development of a fully fledged system in the early years of the twentieth century. However, this chapter will argue that it is the realisations of other countries – the need for legitimation, for a degree of cultural unity, and for a developed economic competitiveness – that are now driving the system in England and Wales at the present time.

Indeed, the lessons of these other countries have not been lost on developing countries today. If Japan is one of the clearest examples of an education system being treated as a tool of national development, it is an example that the 'Asian Tigers' of Singapore, South Korea and Taiwan have taken on board. These 'developmental states' have consistently used education for two major ends. Firstly, and paralleling the inception of earlier systems like Japan, they have used education as a means of constructing national identity and state power. Secondly, however, and now paralleling the growing concerns of Western governments in the second half of the twentieth century, they have used their education systems for developing their economic competitiveness, by intervening to direct and regulate economic activity towards certain specified national ends.

And what of the understanding of teachers in such systems? The problem for teachers is that they are human beings. They are limited both in their lifespan and in their knowledge capacity. They have an average lifespan of less than eighty years, and a working lifespan of little more than forty. Their memories are necessarily short, and their understanding of events world-wide is limited. Understandably, unless they have lived through periods of great change, and are able to compare one regime with another, they will tend to think that what they live under, and perform within, is the norm. The dominant belief of teachers in England and Wales, for instance, who have had at least a dozen years of experience under their belt, regarding the 'proper' role of teaching, will probably be one of professional autonomy. They were, after all, born into, trained for and practised within a system that encouraged a belief in their professional authority, independence and capability. Yet a brief glance at the changing role of headteachers in England and Wales (Table 1.1) would show that their experience was a fairly lengthy but nevertheless transitory phase; and as the speed of change has increased, so their role has changed as rapidly. The first phase lasted for a century, the second phase for thirty to forty years, the third for only ten to fifteen years before apparently being replaced by the present condition.

What this argues then is that, were human beings to have a longer lifespan and a wider experience, teachers would be much more aware of the fact that

Table 1.1 The changing role of the headteacher in England and Wales (1850–2000)

	Key words	Function	Power	Constraints/issues
C 19th head	Hierarchy Moral & cultural transmission Control	Transmission of upper- & middle-class moral and cultural hegemony through school managers and governors Social control	Internally strong, but power set within strong framework Set and monitored by others	Degrees of: Hierarchy & democracy? Social control? Professionalism?
Social Democratic head 1940s–1980s	Cultural autonomy Professional empowerment Innovative potential	Patriarchal leadership Professional domination for either liberal or conservative (not radical) rule	Ideological and professional with possible curricular or organisational innovation Within contemporary value structure	Change dependent on head's personality Circumscribed by contemporary values Financial & resource decisions mostly located elsewhere
Market head 1980s–1990s	Service competition Entrepreneurialism Responsiveness Financial flexibility	Chief executive of institution Determining aims, strategies Building on cultures to service wants and needs of customers All within competitive framework	Determined by ability to service clients' needs To sell a product by maintaining a competitive edge	Are clients consumers or citizens? How do schools contribute to a public good? Are equality issues addressed?
'Outcomes head'	Standards Value-added targets Outcomes Benchmarking	Strategist for implementing external directives Professional manager rather than senior teacher Monitor, evaluator & manager of teacher & pupil standards	Greater pressure & power to dismiss 'failing' teachers Collegiality essential for achievements and standards co-opted by head Emphasis on leadership as key feature	Government policy What is child centredness in this vision? Inspection Role of the professional/Bentham's Panopticon

their experience was not the norm, but a product of very special conditions, peculiar to a particular time and place. However, the danger with this awareness is that it would then be very easy to adopt a relativist position – to argue that because the role of an education system has varied with time and place, and as the role of teachers has similarly varied, so their role should only be defined by an historical context. In other words, any book on teachers' deprofessionalisation is necessarily limited to a particular time and place. Yet this is to commit the naturalistic fallacy, for just because teachers' roles have been determined in the past by the systems they have worked within is no reason to suggest that this is the way it should be.

Indeed, this book will argue that a crucial function of teachers as professionals needs to be their engagement with matters beyond the classroom, as part of a larger picture of citizen education. And this citizen education, as Green (1997, p. 5) argues, needs to be

> ... conscious of the interdependence of nations, the diversity of societies, and the necessarily global nature of solutions to the world's problems, [one that would] eschew the narrow cultural chauvinism which has characterised much of what has passed for national education ... equally, recognising the importance of cohesion and solidarity in modern societies, it would seek to promote new and more inclusive forms of national identity.

This kind of citizen education is necessary not only because it is seen as the best way of equipping students with the knowledge, skills and attitudes necessary to cope with an increasingly chaotic and unpredictable world – the historical context – but also because such an approach is underpinned by a set of principles concerned with the development of democracy, participation, equality and respect, which transcend the situation of a world at the turn of the millennium. Yet for teachers to provide such an education they need these kinds of knowledge, skills, attitudes and principles themselves; and these do not happen if they are seen – and see themselves – as some lower-order technician in an economically determined state hierarchy.

Deprofessionalisation, then, is also a term that has wider currency than any one particular context. Whilst there will necessarily be variation from country to country, the argument here is that the re-conceptualisation of the teaching profession is essential to the development of democratic government – and we believe that this is no parochial concern.

In the present context of what is argued as a period of teachers' deprofessionalism, a little historical background is therefore needed. This background will form the backdrop to developments over the last decade or so, and then lead directly into the kinds of changes that are happening at present. As we have argued, there are clearly particular issues of national culture, political personality, and geographical events which make each system's reaction to wider phenomena fairly individual. Nevertheless, there are supra-national strands which are more important and more intrusive upon national educational policies than in the past. From this kind of picture it will be possible to chart the changing role of the professional, and of the need to conceptualise the educational agenda rather differently from how it is pictured at present. This, then, will be the purpose of this chapter.

Development of recent educational policies

It has already been argued that education systems have normally been seen as pivotal to state formation, legitimacy, cultural unification and, lately, economic and cultural competitiveness. Indeed, as one nation's economic star rises and another's wanes, a standard object of scrutiny has been the strengths and weaknesses of the education systems. Thus, calls for a radical re-think of the US education system occurred after 1961 when the Russians beat the Americans in putting the first man into space. They recurred in the 1970s (Silberman 1973), and again in the 1980s when Japan rose to challenge its economic hegemony, and continued in the 1990s (e.g. Chubb and Moe 1990), and so on to this day, with the rise of Charter schools (Wohlstetter *et al.* 1995). Part of the blame for this parlous state of affairs with the education system was located with the teaching profession, for not gearing their schools to the current needs of society – though it should be noted that some commentators have argued that this was very largely manufactured (e.g. Berliner and Biddle 1995).

In the United Kingdom, whilst issues were raised about the state of education in the 1960s (e.g. the Black Papers), it required the deep financial difficulties generated by the oil crises of the early 1970s to spark off governmental action. Prime Minister Callaghan's 1976 Ruskin College speech asked (i.e. doubted) whether education was providing industry with the workers with training in the basic subject necessities, and unequivocally stated that government needed to be involved in more than the determination of structure and resource allocation. It had, he argued, a responsibility to ensure that what was happening internally was to the advantage of children, parents and the nation as a whole.

A number of implications stemmed from comments like these, and much comment from then on. The first was that an educational system should not be there for the benefit and enjoyment of its producers, but for its recipients, whether these be conceptualised as children, parents, or government and industry. This increase in demands upon 'producers' from both above and below will be seen to be a characteristic of much reform in not only England and Wales, but internationally as well. Thus, systems as varied in form and function as England and Wales, New Zealand, Canada, Australia, the United States, and Sweden began to move towards various forms of increased implementational and financial decentralisation (see Whitty *et al.* 1998). At the same time, these were accompanied by governmental increased control of policy through tighter specification of content and/or output – what Neave (1998) came to call the rise of the 'evaluative state'.

This was a time when governments increasingly came to believe that this 'producer capture' had been the case for far too long, a suspicion of professionals which also ran counter to much of the accepted wisdom until that time. Table 1.2 suggests that for the period from the Second World War, there had been a general consensus that education systems, as so much else of welfare states in Western countries, were in the 'safe' hands of the professionals. Governments, the general public, public service managers, and the professionals themselves saw their welfare state systems as ones that were underpinned by professions who through their expertise had the ability to know what needed to be done; and who through their codes of ethics and altruism could be trusted not only to know what was best, but also would do this as well. They could and should be trusted to perform their crucial social functions in an independent and autonomous manner. This period, from the middle 1940s to the middle 1970s, was, as most commentators on Western educational systems now accept, the golden age of teachers' professional autonomy and public regard. Teachers accepted that governments provided the broad legislative framework for education, but they were crucial in interpreting this framework, and in being the dominant suppliers. In such a system, there were few if any government-specified outputs – these were for

Table 1.2 Steering and rowing – policy changes since the Second World War

	Phase 1	*Phase 2*	*Phase 3*
Approach	Social Democracy.	New Right.	New Modernisers.
Steering?/ Rowing?	Steering and rowing.	No steering, no rowing.	Steering, limited rowing.
Strategy	Government framework, state suppliers, no government standards.	Market framework, market suppliers, market standards.	Government framework, mixed suppliers, government standards.
The role of markets	Markets seen as detrimental to development of educational collaboration, civic development, and enhancement of 'public good'.	Markets seen as natural, moral and economic way of deciding preferences, allocating resources, and achieving efficiencies.	Markets seen as useful means for gingering up implementation of centrally designed policies. Who implements what is immaterial as long as output controls, access, and standards are all defined and monitored.

the professionals to define. Social democratic regimes were essentially concerned with government performing the 'steering' of the education system, the
'rowing' to be largely determined and monopolised by its servants (see
Osborne and Gaebler 1992).

Now it is fairly easy for governments to grant these kinds of concessions to
professional bodies when economies are buoyant, and when there are few
resource constraints. It is also fairly easy when it is believed that the
introduction of such a system will decrease problems, rather than create new
ones. It is also not going to be seen as problematic when governmental
attention is devoted to the building of structures and issues of resource
allocation rather than that of internal practice. Finally, when governments
lack the political will, and believe that they also lack the expertise to know
how to go about determining just how good a job professionals are actually
doing, problems with such a solution are hardly going to loom large.

Yet times change, and when such changes cause difficulties, governments will
take a much harder look at professional practice. Three of these changes will be
mentioned here. Firstly, at an institutional level, it became increasingly
apparent that what happened internally in terms of practices and procedures
was just as important an influence on outcomes as structures. In such
circumstances it is unsurprising that there is a demand for the role of
management to change from a facilitatory to a much more interventionist one.
Secondly, at national level, demographic trends meant that populations became
increasingly older, and as they did so, there was an increasingly declining tax
base to draw on, putting greater pressure on government spending, and upon
the financing of the welfare state – another reason for examining professional
practice. Thirdly, at an international level, competitiveness intensified as
formerly underdeveloped and developing countries became more competitive in
terms of both cheap labour and in the production of finished goods. In such
circumstances, economic growth became that much harder to generate, and yet
again government finances came under pressure. Professional practice, like
much else, would be more closely scrutinised.

The rise of the market

It is not surprising that as long ago as 1977, in a Green Paper, the Labour
government of the United Kingdom made a statement that has increasingly
come to represent the attitudes of governments generally in the provision of
education:

> It would not be compatible with the duties of the Secretaries of State
> to promote the education of the people of England and Wales, or with
> their accountability to Parliament, to abdicate from leadership on
> educational issues which have become a matter of lively public
> concern. (para. 2.19)

This is a very clear statement that the long honeymoon with the teaching profession was over – government would now be interested not just in structures and finance but in practice as well.

It took the advent of a Conservative government under Margaret Thatcher to generate significant educational reform, and then of a form that incorporated very strong New Right market influences, influences that went beyond the United Kingdom. Chubb and Moe (1990), for instance, claim to have drawn huge inspiration for their proposed reforms to the United States from the other side of the Atlantic. These influences have also become important currency beyond the political right, with the concept of an 'internal market' (Enthoven 1985) as well as that of 'Market Socialism' (LeGrand and Estrin 1989) now being concepts seriously debated in all the major political parties throughout the Western world. The introduction and development of competition, and the use of some kind of market to engender it, are now a standard feature of virtually all areas of welfare state provision, including that of education.

In the United Kingdom, Conservative governments were at pains to stress their determination to introduce a market-place in education and to stimulate competition between schools through such policies as creating different kinds of providers (e.g. city technology colleges and grant-maintained schools). The policy was enhanced by increasing the degree of local financial control through devolving high levels of finance to schools by means of the Local Management of Schools (LMS), as well as the expansion of consumer choice through open enrolment for pupil numbers. Greater public accountability, which thereby allowed the consumer to make a more informed choice, was attempted through the provision of data about pupil and school. The market philosophy of education thus sought to empower parents as customers by providing information, opportunities and alternatives, and to make schools more conscious of, and responsive to those they existed to serve.

It was a system, then, that meant that teachers in the public sector had to accept competition from other suppliers, and the increased use of market standards to determine the success and failure of their outputs. If social democracy had favoured steering and rowing, this new ideology, at least in part, espoused a drastic reduction in government steering, and a rowing decided much more by competition between institutions (see Figure I.2). The impact on professional practice was twofold. At the practical level, it meant that schools became much more like businesses or schools in the private sector, for school and job survival depended upon success in the market-place. Creativity was to be encouraged within an entrepreneurial paradigm. The school principal began to look increasingly like a chief executive of a business, the teachers the foot-soldiers in this new exercise. Curricula and teaching methods, where they were not decided at national level, would be increasingly determined by client feedback – the customer might not be always right, but their concerns would necessarily have to play an increasing part in any educational agenda. The days of the Dionysian teacher (Handy 1985), when the school was seen as being there to facilitate the wishes of the professional, were increasingly numbered.

The second impact on professional practice was to re-conceptualise this much more along business lines. There was a hugely increased expansion of management courses and management literature which drew upon the business world for its inspiration. Teachers were exhorted to read Peters and Waterman, Rosabeth Moss Kanter, Peter Drucker, and Charles Handy, not only for the issues they raised, but also for the value framework within which their thoughts were contextualised. And if this business context was not specifically recommended, its use as a framework for educational thinking was certainly not discouraged. The language of business now invaded the teaching lexicon: producers, customers, products, entrepreneurialism, efficiency and effectiveness now replaced teachers, pupils, parents, process, and equity as key concepts. Even quality was re-interpreted and re-processed, now being conceptualised in quantitative terms, and deriving primarily from the work of J. Edwards Deming, an American business thinker writing and working primarily for Japanese industrial concerns.

It is important to note that whilst devolutionary policies were introduced by Conservative governments in the United Kingdom and United States under Thatcher and Reagan, they were introduced by Labour governments in Australia and New Zealand (though in none of these cases were the policies reversed when the opposition parties gained power). Similarly, Pollitt (1992) has described the different approaches to the management of the public sector in the United States and United Kingdom, driven largely by the different political constitutions of the two countries, and the fusing of this with the personalities of Reagan and Thatcher.

Of course, the implementation of legislation and the development of policies are never uniform across countries. As already noted, there is always a mixture of policy direction with the influence of national cultures, government political orientation, and individual personalities. Thus, Gamble (1988) has commented upon the apparently contradictory nature of much Thatcherite legislation; apparently vehement free-market advocacy was accompanied by hugely centralising, even authoritarian agendas. He argued that there was actually a coherence to this, in that to change a system, more must be done than the simple provision of a set of alternatives to those of the state. The desires and expectations of both providers and consumers must also be changed, and to do this support must be given to a new system such that it is a more attractive alternative than that which has gone before. The result in the United Kingdom was an apparently rather contradictory and individualised educational framework. On the one hand there was a parochial, bureaucratic and centralist national curriculum. On the other hand, there was a clear response to a much more international agenda of financial and implementational devolution, framed within a system geared to markets and competition (Caldwell and Spinks 1988).

The rather muddled genesis of the system in England and Wales is almost certainly true; yet the combination of policies of the development of quasi-markets along with self-management, combined with strong centralisation of policy agendas and increased determination of the measurement of producer output, is another very strong characteristic of systems on a world-wide basis. As we shall see, this approach moved from muddle to genuine policy in the United Kingdom. In New Zealand and Australia, financial devolution and self-management have similarly been accompanied by an increased control by means of measurement of output, and in the United States charter schools are given their charter and their freedom only after very clear outputs are specified which they must achieve; failure to do so results in the loss of their charter.

The global context

The increasing international homogeneity of policy direction can be better understood when a further factor is incorporated into the picture so far presented. This factor is that which attended the increased impact of issues of globalisation. Now whilst global influences upon local conditions have been evident in some respects for over a century (Hirst and Thompson 1996), there are issues that have reached their degree of influence and penetration only at this moment in time, because other factors have made them possible. To understand this, one also has to understand that globalisation has many facets. Waters (1995), for instance, argues that there are economic, cultural, and political aspects to the phenomenon – these being mediated in many cases by the ease of transfer of symbolic forms, most notably through dramatically improved communication links. One could argue a strong case for environmental globalisation as well. Pollution and deforestation, for example, are having far wider effects now than at any time previously because of the sheer scale of what is currently occurring. This chapter will, however, concentrate upon economic issues, because it will be argued that this is the area that is having the most profound effects upon policies of governments around the world at the present time, including, unsurprisingly, those in the United Kingdom. These policies increasingly locate education at the centre of government strategy, and therefore have an increasing impact upon the life and work of educators.

The argument, then, goes as follows. There is a developing belief by commentators and policy-makers alike that the nation-state is increasingly circumscribed in its ability to affect economic matters, and effect economic change within its own boundaries (e.g. Reich 1991, Korten 1995, Ohmae 1995, Gray 1998). This reduced ability of the nation-state is predicated upon at least three interrelated understandings. The first is that financial markets are becoming liberated from the constraints of national policy-makers. The second is that nation-states, for reasons of self-interest and external imperatives, are being moved into agreements that locate both economic and political decision-making with supra-national bodies, such as the EC and NAFTA. Finally, trans-national companies (TNCs) now enjoy a considerable ability to play nation-states off against one another in their search for the location that will provide them with the cheapest labour force, the greatest tax breaks, and the best position to penetrate other markets. In such a situation, it is argued, the governments of nation-states are increasingly circumscribed in their ability to effect economic change, for power is located elsewhere, and they must respond to pressures beyond their control. Reich's (1991, p. 1) conclusion is fairly apocalyptic:

> ... There will be no more national products and technologies, no national corporations, no national industries. There will no longer be national economies at least as we have come to understand that term. All that will remain rooted within national borders are the people who comprise the nation. Each nation's primary assets will be its citizens' skills and insights.

National responses

In such situations, then, it is not surprising if the manifestos of different political parties around the world begin to look remarkably similar (as they did for instance in the UK general election in May 1997): they are, after all, faced by the same problems and increasingly the same options by which to respond.

Nevertheless, the situation cannot rest there. A number of commentators (e.g. Brown and Lauder 1997) suggest that nation-states have increasingly sought to take an active rather than a passive role in this economic scenario. On this perspective, the apparent unbridled enthusiasm by the Reagan and Thatcher administrations for the discipline of the market in domestic policies has been re-appraised. Not only did it produce greater disparities of wealth between rich and poor, which many believe led to increased social problems; it also, it is claimed, failed to produce in sufficient quantities the kinds of workforce required for the next millennium. What form will the workforce need to take? Firstly, they will not be cheap: most developing countries can substantially undercut the cheapest imaginable wages of an advanced Western nation. Secondly, they must increasingly be given the skills in those areas in which that particular nation has a competitive advantage – where it can niche-market itself and its products. So, predominantly, they will need to be knowledge, electronic or service workers; an unskilled labour force is simply not an option. Lastly, but crucially, as writers like Ashton and Sung (1997) argue, nation-states cannot afford to sit back and hope that this state of affairs will happen of its own accord. They must shape it; they must proactively bend markets to their advantage.

17

How will this be done? It will involve a number of strategies. It will mean that post-Thatcherite and post-Reagan governments – what will be called 'New Modernist' governments – must and will decide what their nation's principal markets are. It will then involve the government in attracting those TNCs that would best help the nation-state to develop those particular markets. Part of this attraction would be performed in the standard way: tax-breaks, 'sweeteners', preferential loans, etc., but part of the attraction must come from the provision of a workforce that can expertly and effectively service the needs of a preferred TNC. As mentioned, this cannot be left to markets. In an age of constant movement, employers will think twice about investing large amounts in individuals who may well move elsewhere within a matter of a few months and there are always free riders in markets who would deliberately leave it to others to invest in education, while they reap the benefits. In such a situation, it then becomes imperative for governments to invest in education, to develop the human capital to service the needs of TNCs. Education – the state education system – then takes on an even more pivotal role in the generation of wealth creation, seen as fundamental to the financing of other areas of the welfare state. Indeed, in an age when all Western governments face the dilemmas of a decreasing tax base due to an increasingly ageing population, the extra devolution of government time and effort to this wealth creation could well be seen as the crucial role of government, and lack of attention to it as a stark abnegation of duty.

In policy terms, what this will mean is that the dominant priority will be economic. Before political or social objectives, these New Modernist governments must ensure that the right kinds of companies are attracted to their country, and that the educational system is geared to servicing the needs of such an economy, which means equipping a workforce with those skills that are needed in an advanced economy. Such skills are linked to the need for a global strategy, and one that does not leave them to the whims and vagaries of the market. The governmental role is then a directive one, in which it not only frames and implements a human-resources policy for society as a whole, but also uses its powers increasingly to determine the type of business that will be attracted to its market. Low-skill, low-wage occupations are discouraged. As the United Kingdom's National Commission on Education said in 1993 (p. 33): 'competition and low-cost global communications, no country like ours will be able to maintain its standard of living, let alone improve it, on the basis of cheap labour and low-tech products and services'.

This will then mean an emphasis on the skills of the technological, the literate and numerate. There will then be a perceived need to have a workforce on the cutting edge of information technology, to supply the kinds of skills that information-age companies will require. A national workforce of this kind will also need to be literate and numerate, for in such a society the unskilled are the unemployable; a burden on the nation, and a social problem waiting to happen.

With this kind of agenda, it is no accident that the Foreword by the UK Secretary of State for Education and Employment David Blunkett to his Green Paper *The Learning Age* (1998) begins:

> Learning is the key to prosperity – for each of us as individuals, as well as for the nation as a whole. Investment in human capital will be the foundation of success in the knowledge-based global economy of the twenty-first century. This is why the Government has put learning at the heart of its ambition.

This rationale for learning is openly technical–rationalist, economic and reductionist; it provides no other reasons for why learning might be a good other than its economic usefulness. Even when it continues, it unproblematically locates notions of creativity and imagination within the same agenda:

> ... This Green Paper sets out for consultation how learning throughout life will build human capital by encouraging the acquisition of knowledge and skills and emphasising creativity and imagination. The fostering of an enquiring mind and the love of learning are essential to our future success ... (ibid.)

New Modernisers and the market

So far, the picture is reasonably clear and straightforward. The 1990s have continued to see a re-ordering and subjugation of new-right agendas to one much more centralising and controlling, yet more pragmatic and ideological. Management agendas in schools are now even more directed from the centre, in terms of curriculum, assessment, and professional development. Using Osborne and Gaebler's metaphor again (1992), whilst government accepts that there can be much more limited rowing by the state and its employees, it vigorously re-asserts the steering characteristic of social democracy, and extends it. As Marquand said of New Labour in the United Kingdom (1998, p. 21): 'It rests on the premise that government at the centre not only can, but should remake society to fit an *a priori* grand design.' This new approach – which will be called the New Modernisers approach – is, then, a departure from new-right theories, but it does not necessarily mean a return to the principles of social democracy.

In this respect, it is instructive to look at the thinking exhibited by Marcel Masse (1996), the Canadian Liberal Minister for Public Service Renewal:

> Ten years ago we still lived under the idea that the government was God-like and thus expected to solve all problems ... In the final analysis, government wasn't always the best vehicle to provide some

services . . . we are heading towards establishing what I call a 'core government' whose essential role is to develop policies that can be adapted quickly to meet changing needs.

This could have been said by a representative of the previous UK Conservative government, or indeed by a member of the Clinton administration. However, whilst all would espouse the reduction of red tape, the empowerment of staff, and greater decentralisation, the previous UK government would have been much more interested in the use of the private sector, and of markets in particular, to generate desired change. New Moderniser thinking, however, is underpinned more by the thinking of Osborne and Gaebler (1992), which espouses an entrepreneurialism, but one located within the public sector, as well as the increased use of new public management techniques (Bottery 1998), which result in a managerial revolution within the public sector, rather than a movement from the public to the private. The new right opened up the debate about the legitimate role of the state, and argued that by invoking the use of markets, it should be as restricted as possible. New Modernisers, however, see the consequences of the market as increases in crime, poverty, and a growing gap between the rich and the poor, in which the rich withdraw behind their gated communities. Rather, they see from the government little more than an abnegation of responsibility. New Modernisers do not argue against the existence of markets *per se*, but rather the intrusion of markets into what is necessarily the province of government. Markets, then, need to be seen as means to ends, not as ideological ends in themselves. For New Modernisers, government should be efficient, entrepreneurial and accountable, but it should not be marginal. It has a key role to play, and it must be done better.

The departure of Reagan and Bush, Thatcher and Major, and the arrival of Clinton and Blair, then, have been the cause of a number of major policy changes. In the Western world generally, governments are distancing themselves from the anti-governmentalism of the 1980s and early 1990s. The desire to maintain the legitimacy of the state is being combined with a view of entrepreneurialism that, rather than locating this within a private agenda, sees it just as much in unleashing the creativity of those in the public sector. As Guy Peters (1995, p. 313) put it: 'The assumption is that the public interest would be better served by a more active and interventionist public sector, and that collective action is part of the solution and not part of the problem.'

Managed markets, central direction, and the 'third way'

This chapter has already detailed the perceived requirement of new economic strategies caused by global developments, as well as the role of markets in a subordinate and controlled role. Markets, then, may be seen as only one part of a larger post-Fordist strategy, consisting of two distinct but complementary parts. First, markets may be seen as a means to increase the 'productivity' and responsiveness of teachers and others in the public sector, through the encouragement among them of a more entrepreneurial attitude, and through the threat of the negative side of market logic – the loss of one's job if one does not compete well enough. The market, then, is not, as free marketeers would like it to be, the defining characteristic of how the service is run, but merely a means to an end, and a carefully circumscribed means at that. For the second and dominant aspect of this strategy is that of a strong central hold on policy direction. This requirement by governments is increasingly seen as inevitable in the light of global competition, ageing populations, and continued and unsustainable demands upon welfare services. In the light of this, governments have had to devise means of reducing such demand, of cutting back services, specifying for efficiency's sake the ways in which money will be spent, and then of increasing their scrutiny of the manner in which this money is spent. Unsurprisingly, perhaps, professionals who might like to think that one of their defining characteristics is that of autonomy, will be less and less tolerated if they resist such central strategic direction for their practice and purpose.

Now if one examines what a real market in education would look like, a thoroughgoing one that resembled a market in business would require a number of features if it were to qualify, and it could easily be seen that public provision of education in the United Kingdom does not conform very closely to these features, nor has there been significant movement towards this realisation since the major Thatcherite reforms of the late 1980s. Perhaps, however, the crucial realisation is not that markets in education have failed to develop to the same extent as those in the private sector, but rather that the development of markets *per se* is not seen as a problem for New Modernisers, as long as, and using the metaphor of steering and rowing described in Table 1.2, these markets are developed only for improving the rowing of the boat of state, not for its steering. Markets then can be encouraged for the implementation of policy, but not for its determination. Thus, to take an example, whilst private ownership of state schools has not been too seriously entertained by any major political party in the United Kingdom, yet as long as sufficient guidelines and output controls were placed over the running of such institutions, and access to them was provided by means of some kind of educational voucher, the privatisation of schools, for New Modernisers at least, would not be seen as a problem. New Modernisers would feel, after all, that they were in control of educational strategy and policy; who implemented it might be a matter of small concern if output controls were in place, access was widened, and standards were achieved.

In the light of these developments, the dominance of the new-right mantras – the prioritisation of individual needs and desires over communal ones – is being re-thought, with inevitable consequences for educational policy and practice. This re-thinking – essentially an attempt at borrowing from liberal and social democratic traditions to create a synthesis that justifies state intervention whilst protecting individual freedom – is essentially the much-vaunted project of the 'third way'. Now it is clear from what has gone above that one half of the project – state intervention – is very clearly in place, and professionals, and teachers in particular, are feeling the force of this strongly. But what of the other half – the protection of individual freedom? How might one assess the strength of this half? There would seem to be a number of ways of judging this. First would be by means of looking at the social and moral educational agenda of a government – the way they approach this would seem to be a strong pointer to their intentions. Second would be to examine the approach to questions of equality – for policies (or lack of them) to realise greater equality would again spell out policy aspirations. And finally, an examination of the reality of the development of citizenship would also help to determine what is really happening *vis-à-vis* individual liberties. Once these are examined, one can begin to ascertain the actual balance between state intervention and individual liberty in 'third way' policies, and secondly, one can go on to develop a good idea of what kind of role teachers will be asked to play in this.

The social and moral agenda, and the 'third way'

A number of commentators (e.g. Green 1997) have commented that whilst state formation and the creation of a national, cultural and civic consciousness was the primary aim of the first state educational systems, yet as these became less urgent, less problematic, so these concerns tended to decline in importance. Certainly, in Western countries (unlike the Asian Tigers and other Newly Industrialised Countries (NICs)) there has been a general decline in the centrality of civic and moral education concerns when compared with the economic. Yet in many ways, present conditions hark back to these earlier days. With the increased pressures upon the nation-state, with the increasing cultural diversity and differentiation within the nation itself, the problems of unity and legitimacy are issues of real concern once again. Thus, it could well be argued that a time has been reached when education systems need to be as concerned with the affective, the social and moral, as they are with the cognitive and skill-based.

Indeed, in terms of skills, the social and moral will be just as important as the intellectual and practical. Whilst the workers of the twenty-first century will not be anything like the worker of the Victorian factory, there will still be a need to socialise the workforce to the kind of work they will be undertaking. In a world of constant change, where people must interface with others, where social cohesion is more important for societal health than the promotion of self-regarding individualism, workers will need to be team players who understand hierarchy and responsibility, who accept the need for flexibility, and who are creative within an entrepreneurial, single-loop environment.

They are to be consulted through techniques like TQA (for that improves the rowing, the implementation of the final product) but they are not to participate (for that is decided by those steering the boat, the policy-makers). On this agenda, the personal and social curricula of schools will be located away from notions of a morality and social behaviour autonomously arrived at by means of rational discussion and reflection, towards ones based much more upon a specification of desirable character traits – virtues – and then to the training of children in these from an early age.

This is an approach that has been widely advocated in the United States (see Lickona 1991, Kilpatrick 1992), and has received, through the populist writings of Etzioni (1993) increasing support on this side of the Atlantic. Whilst the specification of such character traits can include ones such as criticality, justice, and the pursuit of equality and reason, and whilst rational methods can be utilised in their dissemination, the very move away from the kinds of moral education approaches advocated by Kohlberg in the United States and by McPhail and Wilson in the United Kingdom allows for the specification of a character education much more in keeping with the kind of global economic individual described above. If this is the case, then notions of responsibility, duty, respect and perseverance, diligence, moderation, and a positive work ethic may spring more readily to mind.

Besides demands for the incorporation of a social and moral agenda into an economic one, there is also the pressing requirement, as seen by some policy-makers, for the regeneration of a social and moral agenda because of the perceived breakdown in society. When Lickona wrote (1991, p. 19) that

> ... everyone is concerned about the breakdown of the family; everyone is concerned about the negative impact of television on children; everyone is concerned about the growing self-centredness, materialism and delinquency they see among the young ...

he was echoing the thoughts of many. And whilst Etzioni might argue (1997, p. xvii) that '... societies have lost their equilibrium, and are heavily burdened with antisocial consequences of excessive liberty' there seems a much more general acceptance that societal breakdown, such as it is, is as much to do with the use of unfettered markets at national level, particularly by the Thatcher and Reagan administrations, as it is to do with the inheritance of the 'swinging sixties'. Yet whilst it may have rather different roots, it appears to end up with the same kinds of calls: a need for a greater sense of shared value, of community, and of responsibility by the individual to the society within which they live. As argued above, it would be surprising if governments did not incorporate such concerns into their plans for education. But certainly, on these terms, social and moral agendas would fit much more comfortably into the state-interventionist and state-directed half of the 'third way' than on the personal-liberty side.

If a country moved further down a road that incorporated a social and moral agenda into an economic one, and adopted a variation of the character-education approach apparently so popular in many school systems in the United States, a number of benefits might transpire. Firstly, there might be a harder realisation that moral relativism is not an option for a policy agenda. No society admits, nor can it afford to admit, that all behaviours and practices are of similar worth or value, and a necessary debate would then be initiated which asked 'what are the core values that this society needs to uphold?'. Paradoxically, there would also be a more general recognition that groups within even the most multicultural society tend to share rather similar sets of values. A third benefit might be the recognition that rights and responsibilities are symbiotic: in particular, that the wide enjoyment of rights is predicated upon the existence of a healthy and flourishing society, and this requires an attitude of responsibility to community and society. Finally, it may generate a greater – Aristotelian – understanding that social and moral development are practical processes, which are only properly realised by doing and living them; an understanding that would profoundly affect the way in which schools planned and implemented a curriculum in this area.

Such an approach has its down side. For, firstly, the linking of social and moral agendas to the economic devalues the individual self-chosen path if it is not entrepreneurially inclined; there will be little consideration given to those who have other views of what the good society might comprise. As social and moral values become the handmaidens of economic policy, views, opinions and interests beyond this paradigm are demoted and disadvantaged. Secondly, as certain virtues are adopted and others downgraded in the search for what are the 'core' communal values, it seems likely that some values, and sets of values, will be downgraded as others are presented as those of the 'community'. A final and related but wider danger is that of illiberalism. If a communal set of values is debated, and then adopted as 'official', then there is the danger that democracy is interpreted as meaning nothing more than the rule of the majority. The adoption of a set of dominant communal values does not sit well with a belief in the tolerance of a variety of different beliefs, for from it may develop an intolerance of minority perspectives.

The equality agenda

There has not been a great deal in policy statements by New Labour in the United Kingdom that specifically addresses questions of equality, raising the real possibility that such issues will be ignored, or inadequately supported, and thereby decreasing any specific commitment to issues of positive liberty and freedom to do things. There could be at least two reasons for this, neither of which could be counted as adequate. A first is a 'jam tomorrow' kind of argument. This would suggest that problems of equality of opportunity can be dealt with only when the country is in a sufficiently strong economic position such that it has the extra capital to spend on such programmes. This underpins one of the arguments to which George and Miller (1994) refer when they describe debates about the scope of the welfare state provision. These, they suggest, have moved from ones of universal welfare provision, enthusiastically supported at the time of welfare state inception, through to new-right suggestions that, for reasons of self-reliance as much as financial pressures, provision should be no more than residual. As noted above, however, the ideological high-water mark of Thatcher and Reagan has passed, and George and Miller argue that we have entered a new, more pragmatic phase, in which welfare-state provision is seen as a praiseworthy objective, but only to be provided when it can be afforded. From such an argument stem 'jam tomorrow' approaches, for whilst the United Kingdom faces the economic difficulties that it does, extra spending on welfare that does not directly support economic agendas must be very largely an issue for the future. The problem with this is not only that it is not always clear when sufficient resources will be available for this extra provision; it is also a case of political will as well as financial calculation. To put it bluntly, money may be found for those things that matter to government, and a 'jam tomorrow' argument leaves the flexibility for governments to slip out of such commitments and to spend such money on more vote-winning and populist endeavours. Finally, and perhaps most crucially, a 'jam tomorrow' approach does not address the fact that whilst questions of equality are delayed until financial calculations and political will decide that such investment is possible, those suffering continue to be deprived of those things to which they should have access, not only because they are citizens of that country and therefore deserve access equal to any other citizen, but also as a matter of common morality: suffering by its nature should be alleviated.

This first 'jam tomorrow' reaction is inadequate, but it does at least signal a commitment to become further involved in redressing questions of inequality at some stage. A second reason for current lack of action on issues of equality of opportunity should cause rather more concern. This would be the view that questions of inequality are resolved – or at least the government's responsibility for dealing with them are resolved – by making sure that everyone who is willing to work, has the opportunity of getting a job and is ensured of 'employability'. This would fit well with strategies that adopted the Singaporean, niche-marketing approach: if government ensured that schools, as well as further and higher education, were all re-focused such that they equipped individuals with the kinds of skills that will be required to service a selected range of companies, then the provision of the education to acquire a decent job, an adequate income and a reasonable standard of living, it might be argued, was all that was required to resolve the question of government's responsibility for dealing with questions of equality. This however would be grossly inadequate – issues of racism, sexism, and ageism do not cease to be factors in employment just because someone has got adequate qualifications, just as issues of positive liberty need a firm commitment to personal empowerment. Even Giddens' vision of a 'Social Investment State' (1998, p. 117) to replace the Welfare State ('... investment in human capital wherever possible, rather than the direct provision of economic maintenance') does not seem quite to close the gap between skill provision and overt action to reduce instances of discrimination and inequality. There is, then, the genuine possibility that if action to deal with issues of equality is neglected, questions of positive liberty may be similarly neglected.

The citizenship agenda

If what has gone before holds water, then large questions must also be raised about the kind of citizenship that is being envisaged, and the kind that will be provided. This approach, then, has the potential seriously to undermine pluralist perspectives generally, and the strong kinds of participative democracy, advocated initially in Ancient Greece, and more recently by writers like Pateman (1970) and Barber (1984) will not be possible. After all, a post-Fordist state is predicated upon the idea of those at the centre determining policies, whilst the role of others in the policy process is to implement them. This does not mean that there will be no consultation, but consultation does not mean participation. Government has no need to act upon the wishes of those consulted. So in terms of having a plurality of opinions and advice feeding into the decision process, there is no reason to believe that decisions will not have been made at some time previously, and consultation only the political window-dressing.

This also does not bode well for the role of professionals and other bodies. As Pollitt (1992) put it, the situation moves from one where professionals have been 'on top' to one where they are only 'on tap'; their expertise used, and dispensed with, as and when thought necessary. For teachers, it will mean that like the rest of the population, they will increasingly be at the receiving end of the policy process, and regardless of the place of the market in this process, they will be increasingly viewed and treated as producers and customers, not as citizens. So it is for example, that the 'Citizens' Charter' of the Tory government in the United Kingdom, which was carried on by New Labour, is in actuality little more than a customers' charter. For under this charter, if recipients do not get the services to which they are entitled, then a number of things can lead to remediation of the situation. All well and good but this does effectively neutralise the critical, political voice. It leaves little or no room for participation in the conception and formulation of the service, and suggests that citizenship consists of little more than the right to complain if services are not up to scratch. Only at the end of a period of office is a population allowed to express its wish about such issues as conception and formulation, and then policies by different political parties, due to the kinds of globalised pressures described above, increasingly come to resemble one another.

So if citizenship is increasingly defined and reduced to consumership, issues of equality are inevitably raised. At the broadest level, equality of participation in the political process is radically reduced; those who share the policy designs of the party in power, those who are invited to contribute, will be allowed into the policy-making fold, but actual and genuine debate by a plurality of voices which could affect the policy-making process is virtually ruled out. This also means that those avenues for raising issues of inequality by and for various minority groups in society are increasingly designed to be only cosmetic, are discouraged by reductions in funding, or are simply not taken seriously – unless they raise issues that government for one reason or another has decided need to be on the policy agenda.

And citizenship education? Well, certainly, responsibilities and duties will be highlighted quite as much as rights. This is no bad thing in itself, but it has already been suggested that this can become part of a larger, economic agenda, rather than as a principled political attempt to revive a genuinely communal, participatory society. And as citizenship is increasingly defined as consumership, one can expect citizenship education to become more concerned with the ways in which the citizen accesses particular services, and is shown the procedures by which they can choose between providers, or complain about the standard they have received.

The role of the professional

It should be clear by now where professionals fit into all of this. Yet, professional disbelief in the manner in which government – and public – increasingly treats them, suggests that whilst professionals may understand how they are treated, they do not necessarily understand why. The history of the US and UK literature on professionals very much explains the history of their role in the eyes of the public and government, and it is important for this to be understood.

Thus, from being given a mantle by writers like Durkheim (1957) as the much-needed conscience of an increasingly industrialised, business-oriented and value-less world, the literature moves to portraying them as paragons of virtue, through a concentration on great men of a profession (usually medical: see Carr-Saunders and Wilson 1933). This picture lasted for some time, and was, as we have seen, given a boost by the creation of welfare states which were pictured as being serviced by professional bodies in the manner they felt most suitable. Thus, when Friedrich Hayek wrote *The Road to Serfdom* in 1944, arguing that welfare states could lead only to authoritarian government and a dependency culture, he was very much a lone voice. It took an increasingly unstable world and an accompanying sceptical academic literature to question professionals' right to conduct their practice in the way they best thought it should. Forty years on, Hayek's opinions were centre-stage. His views found natural allies in the writings of at least three different groups of writers. The first group, sociologists like Randall Collins (1990), argued that professionals, like any other group of workers, were essentially concerned with the achievement of 'occupational closure'; a desire to place out of limits certain areas of work so that other groups were not allowed to practise, and in so doing to corner a market for themselves, with all the implications this has for job security, autonomy, and wage levels, and for client service and responsiveness. This then forms strong conceptual links with the second group, public-choice theorists like Tullock (1976), Downs (1967) or Niskanen (1971), who argued that bureaucratic power has increased by serving itself rather than the public interest. The third group in effect suggests the solution to the first two groups' criticisms, advocating a market-based approach to the provision of services. Writers from the radical liberal right (e.g. Friedman 1962, Green 1987) were increasingly complemented by writers from the left of the political spectrum (Le Grand and Estrin 1989); both sides came to argue that the provision of services will be improved by the generation of competition between providers. This view in many ways culminates in the views of Osborne and Gaebler (1992), who suggest that whilst government should continue to do the 'steering' of policy, who does the 'rowing' of that policy is fairly irrelevant; whether it is public or private providers is immaterial if they fulfil the standards set by central government (Table 1.2).

During the middle 1990s the combination of centralisation and free markets was no longer seen by policy makers in Western developed countries as necessarily one of contradiction, as long as each was clearly defined (see Smyth 1993). Policy is defined at the centre, and the periphery is given the job of implementing this policy. Further, and most importantly, such post-Fordist approaches mesh exceptionally well with the demands made upon governments by – and their responses to – the kinds of global changes described above. If governments come to the conclusion that they must be proactive, and steer markets, enticing favoured TNCs, and supplying a suitably qualified workforce through a carefully orchestrated education and training strategy, then a strategy that reflects their need to control whilst at the same time utilising markets in a subsidiary role, is going to fit perfectly.

And the professionals? The key words for them under the previous market system were those of competition, entrepreneurialism and institutional survival. Now will be added words like outcomes, standards, and bench-marking. It is clear from this that the increased demands from above and below will mean that school principals must increasingly be managers and overseers rather than senior teachers in a loosely coupled collegiate. As Whitty et al. (1998, p. 51) put it, school principals will now need to 'engage both with the demands of the evaluative state in terms of meeting centrally determined objectives and with the day-to-day "business" of running their school and ensuring its survival within the education market'. Further, the teacher will need to be re-cast as a technical–rationalist implementer rather than a determiner of local needs and appropriate remediation. Collegiality, such as it is, will increasingly look like Hargreaves' (1994) 'contrived collegiality' rather than the genuine participative collegiality that he recommends. It will also mean that within the school there must be a much greater goal orientation than previously. There can now be little time for smelling flowers along the way; the agenda, set months and years in advance, is cast in tablets of stone, and must be achieved if the school is not to face a deluge of inspection and further external interference and control. Finally, there will then necessarily be a greater cultural and interest divide between the school principals and their staff. If one adds to this the continued constrained communication with other schools as they struggle to survive in an educational market-place, the final implication is one of increased pressure and stress upon the individual at the head of the school, and the alienation of the teachers. As governments increasingly espouse a management literature that sees the principal in an heroic and pivotal mould, and as inspection reports increasingly stress the primacy of good leadership in the search for more effective and efficient schools, one can expect increasing evidence of early retirements, increased stress, and slower take-up of such senior management positions.

What then is the role of the teacher in a global world? This chapter has argued that the policy approach of most governments is one of attempting to create a limited, technical–rationalist implementationalist, and institutionally focused professional. What is the reality in schools? Will teachers increasingly become:

- The bureaucratic professional: with the need in a 'rational' world for the systematising, co-ordinating, control and planning of work for the efficiency, effectiveness and economy of the organisation, will teachers be incorporated into organisational purposes, to be 'on tap' rather than 'on top'?
- The free-market teacher: with the encouragement of competition between rival 'firms' of schools, will teachers be made to be more responsive and more efficient, their autonomy ultimately dependent upon clients' perceptions and wishes?
- The post-Fordist teacher: through tight control of policy by the centre, with accompanying devolution of responsibility for implementation of policy to the periphery, will the role of teachers be one of devising policies for making the packaging of their product more competitive than that of the 'firm' down the road, but with the product specified elsewhere?

Which of these three scenarios – if any – is the most likely? The next chapter will begin the attempt to answer this question. In particular it will examine the provision of in-service education for teachers' professional development in the United Kingdom, and provide evidence of the extent to which markets have been allowed to flourish in this significant area of educational provision, or whether central control has had a more central part to play. The examination of in-service education is also a key area in the investigation of the possibilities of teacher deprofessionalisation. This is because what teachers and schools choose to examine, and what they are directed towards, as materials for continuing professional development have a very important impact upon them. This is not only in terms of their conception of what it means to be a 'professional', but also in terms of their ability to understand and deal with constrictions upon their autonomy, and upon their capacity to deal with the kinds of changes detailed above. It is to this topic that the next chapter turns.

2

CENTRAL DIRECTION, MARKETS, AND THE IN-SERVICE EDUCATION OF TEACHERS

Introduction: the rhetoric of market education

When Friedrich Hayek wrote his book *The Road to Serfdom* in 1944, arguing that Communism and Fascism were in actual fact not that different, because they both sought to centralise power in the hands of the few, and that social democracies were proceeding down that very same road, he was a prophet out of his time. They had all abandoned, he argued, 'that freedom in economic affairs without which personal and political freedom has never existed in the past' (ibid., p. 10). The institution of welfare-state legislation in the quest for greater equality, he believed, 'necessarily leads to a greater transformation of the spontaneous order of free society into a totalitarian system conducted in the service of some coalition of organised interests' (1973, p. 2). Yet few were prepared to listen to him. In Britain, major recessions and high levels of unemployment in the 1930s, as well as the sacrifices of a world war, followed by an overwhelming Labour victory at the general election of 1945, led even the mainstream of the Conservative Party to accept the necessity of an interventionist state.

Times change. Thirty years later, the effects of oil price rises in the 1970s, recessions in most Western economies, and the apparent inability of Keynesian economics to deal with them, led a UK Labour government in 1976 to the adoption of the monetarist economic remedies prescribed by the IMF, and an increasing acceptance of the need for the introduction of competitive systems into the workings of the welfare state to cope with the widely acknowledged bureaucratisation, lack of incentives, and provider-led bias. They were not alone; around the world, Hayek, and other academics advocating a radical liberal, market system in public provision (e.g. Friedman 1962, Graham and Clarke 1986, Green 1987) found themselves the principal guests at the party rather than the uninvited looking in. Their ideas have been increasingly accepted beyond the confines of the political Right: the concept of an 'internal market' (Enthoven 1985), as well as that of 'Market Socialism' (LeGrand and Estrin 1989) are now concepts that are debated seriously in all the major political parties throughout the Western liberal democracies. The introduction and development of competition, and the use of some kind of markets to engender it, will be, for the foreseeable future, a standard feature of all areas of welfare-state provision, including that of education.

In the UK, throughout the late 1980s and most of the 1990s, Conservative governments were at pains to stress their determination to introduce a market-place in education and to stimulate competition between schools. This was evidenced by policies to create different kinds of providers, such as city technology colleges and grant-maintained (GM) schools. The policy was enhanced further by increasing the degree of local financial control through devolving high levels of finance (now over 90% in the LEA sector) to schools through the Local Management of Schools (LMS), as well as by the expansion of consumer choice through open enrolment for pupil numbers. These policies have not been changed by the incoming New Labour Government; rather than rein in the freedoms of the grant-maintained schools, legislation for greater financial de-regulation has made local authority schools more like the GM sector than the other way round.

Further, greater public accountability, which thereby allowed the consumer to make a more informed choice, was also attempted through provision of data about pupil and school performance, Standardised Assessment Tasks (SATs) scores in National Curriculum Assessments and tests, and league tables for performance in public examinations at GCSE and 'A' level. This has not changed under a change of government. If anything it has intensified. Finally, the market philosophy in education is also seen in the continued attempt to empower parents as customers by providing information, opportunities and alternatives, and to make schools more conscious of, and responsive to, those they exist to serve.

The market philosophy is also still to be found elsewhere in education, for in the arrangements for initial teacher training, schools bargain with higher education institutions concerning the costs of student placements. Inspection contracts also go out to tender along with the window cleaning and other services that schools may require. By introducing the discipline of the market, the aim has been to transform schools into both consumers of services as well as providers of a service – education for pupils.

The bottom line of a fully implemented market philosophy would be that the good schools (however they are defined) would prosper, the weak and failing would prove so unpopular that through lack of market demand, results publication, and poor inspection performances, they would be closed down. The Conservative Party at the end of July 1995 announced precisely this for the following autumn term at Hackney Downs School (*Observer*, 22.7.95). The new Labour Government has similarly begun the introduction of 'hit squads', teams of experts who will take over the management of failing schools. Some might interpret a number of cases (e.g. The Ridings School in Calderdale, and Perronet Thompson School in Hull), as examples of this, for they have been closed down, and re-opened under new leadership.

Now clearly there are problems with an aggressive market philosophy. Downes (1994), for example, suggested that the major weakness of a market philosophy in education was that 'schools do not fail and close down rapidly; during which time hundreds of children may have received a substandard education which *is the only one* they get' (p. 55, his italics). The issue is probably one of pragmatic balance; achieving a responsiveness and energy whilst not condemning those in failing schools to a 'sink school' experience. This is probably a better description of the three schools described above. However, it is a question of balance. Market provision, and much of the philosophy behind it, is apparently here for the foreseeable future. It is here not only to empower parents in their choice of schools, but also to empower schools *vis-à-vis* the services they need.

The market and INSET

In terms of in-service education and training (INSET) provision, a market may serve some considerable good for schools. Rather than topics being predicated purely upon central government directives, or upon a diet of 'we've always addressed these topics', a vigorous market in in-service education would allow a greater flexibility of choice to the 'consumers' – in this case the schools themselves, and thereby aid them in developing an in-service programme for teachers which moves them towards an ecologically orientated professionalism.

Indeed, there seems little doubt that INSET is an area apparently designed to empower schools in the determination of their own development and ethos. Here the aim of the market discipline has been to break the stranglehold of the providers and give the consumer, in this case the school, the whip hand. Thus, INSET provision in England and Wales has changed dramatically in the last decade. Long secondments for individual teachers and 'pool funding' arrangements, by which a general diet was provided beyond the control of individual schools, have both become a thing of the past. At the same time, five 'Baker days' were introduced in 1987. This meant a change to teachers' contracts; from now on they were required to attend for these five 'non-contact' days and schools had the specific duty of providing INSET for their teachers during that time. Further legislation changed the nature of INSET provision whereby the proportion determined and funded according to national priorities was increased and that determined according to local priorities reduced. The changes produced a plethora of acronyms: TRIST (TVEI Related In-service Training), GRIST (Grant Related In-service Training), LEATGS (LEA Training Grants Scheme) and GEST (Grants for Education Support and Training), details of which can be found in Oldroyd and Hall (1991). The aim of many of these reforms was to break the producer stranglehold on provision at the local-authority level and to increase the ability of schools to act as purchasers of INSET. At the same time, there appears to have been an increase in in-service education and training in the growth of providers, private consultants, LEA teams and higher education lecturers, offering training packages differentially priced to attract a market.

All of this was accompanied by a considerable rhetoric concerning a government-led policy to produce a market in educational services in general, and more competition among providers for the in-service market in particular, as funds were now devolved to schools (and continue to be), and in-service provision reaches more teachers (though for a shorter time per teacher) than of old. There are a number of questions, however, which need to be asked about this policy. A most obvious one is simply to ask to what extent is a market operative in education. Applying this question specifically to INSET provision it would simply ask:

1   To what extent is the market determining what INSET is chosen by schools?

A further related question stems from the fact that the philosophy predicts that, if the market is working, there should be a greater diversity of provision. This being the case it can be asked:

2   Is there greater choice in provision, such as in terms of areas covered, and in terms of length of course?

Pure market theory is based upon notions of equal entry – and hence equal competition in the market. So a further question can be asked:

3   Is there equal or differential access to the market?

From these questions, it is possible to ask whether the market model is an appropriate one to describe what is happening in INSET at the present time, and education in general. The answers to these questions will have considerable bearing upon questions about the development of education for teachers. At the moment, the question is one framed largely in terms of central direction versus market direction in in-service education, though as indicated previously, a combination of the two, in terms of a post-Fordist model, may be a more accurate description of the reality.

Whichever model is the closest fit to the reality for INSET will provide important clues about the model being proposed for teacher professionalism. As well, it must be asked whether there is not another, more appropriate model, which teachers might adopt for their in-service education, for the data provided here do not directly address the normative question of whether, or to what extent, a market, or centralised dictation, or a post-Fordist scenario, should be operative in in-service education. It is with all of these questions, then, empirical, theoretical, and normative, that this chapter is concerned.

Research rationale

The research described in this chapter examines perceptions of the influence of the market philosophy in generating in-service choice in a sample of English secondary schools from three different sectors: the LEA maintained, the grant maintained and independent. It was deliberately decided to approach a sample from each of these three sectors for the following reasons. The LEA-maintained sector was included as it was schools in this sector that, arguably, have been the most reluctant to accept the introduction of a market philosophy. The grant-maintained sector, on the other hand, was expressly created through the 1988 Education Reform Act to bring into being schools whose management would wish to take on more responsibility for their own management, and therefore would be more amenable to a market situation. Their creation would also, it was planned, engender greater competition and choice between schools. The independent sector has always had to operate within a market context, as their clients are parents who choose to pay to send their children to such schools. The schools in this sector, then, ought to have been experienced in dealing in a market situation.

The research began with a letter, with an attached questionnaire, addressed to the school's headteacher, requesting that either he/she or the member of staff with delegated responsibility for oversight of in-service arrangements reply to the questionnaire. This questionnaire was devised to facilitate easy completion and at the same time elicit substantial and significant information. There was a two-thirds response rate by the schools in each of the sectors: in total 87 replies were received, 28 LEA schools, 28 GM schools and 31 independent schools. As well as asking for data about pupil rolls and numbers of teaching staff, the principal inquiries focused on the five following areas.

1 The average length of INSET courses attended and why this length of course had been chosen by the school. This information facilitated the assessment of the prediction that if a market was operating, there should be a greater variety of provision in some kinds of schools than others.
2 The key areas for INSET provision identified in the school management plan for the previous two years. These data helped clarify whether (as market theory would predict) provision was determined by market forces or other external (e.g. legislative) or internal demands. It also facilitated an assessment of whether there was a diversity between sectors.
3 What schools believed would be the key areas of INSET for the coming two years. This allowed an assessment of whether market influence was increasing and also yielded evidence of whether diversity was diminishing or increasing.
4 Perceptions of sources of pressure for INSET choices; whether these were felt to be driven by external or internal pressures or by a combination of both.

5   The strength of influence that schools perceived for nine different areas of
     pressure on their INSET priorities for the present, and which were
     anticipated for the coming two years.

The data

Pupil rolls and number of staff

The basic data indicated that independent schools had the lowest pupil–
teacher ratio (11.6), followed by GM schools (15.9), and then by LEA schools
(17.0). Clearly, if pupil–teacher ratio is a 'selling' factor for schools, then the
independent and GM schools are better placed to attract clients than the LEA
schools. However, one has to be careful here; there are other factors that
attract clients such as quality of the school environment and facilities, and it
would need further evidence on the schools' performance and provision, as
well as the relative financial resources and spending in these areas, before any
firm conclusions could be reached.

Length of in-service courses

If a key feature of a market situation is the ability and the opportunity for
purchasers to make the important decisions – for them to set the agenda – then
one way of assessing this is to investigate the length of INSET courses chosen
by schools and the reasoning for this. A greater degree of market influence,
then, would be indicated by a diversity of choice for schools in the lengths of
courses. The data for course length is given in Table 2.1.

The most striking point about the data in Table 2.1 is the almost complete
domination of the use by schools of the one-day course, indicated by 91% of
respondents. This, initially at least, is not good support for the influence of the
market. When the reasons for choosing this were examined, by means of an
open-response question (Table 2.2), this thesis was substantiated.

It is clear from the data that three major criteria were used: what providers
offered; the cost/time involved; and the disruption caused by such courses. It is
also clear that each sector reacted differently. Thus, cost and time constraints
(37%) were the strongest influences in the LEA-maintained sector. This is not
too surprising, given that budgetary constraints were and continue to be

Table 2.1 Length of in-service course chosen

Course length	LEA (n = 28)	GM (n = 28)	Independent (n = 31)	Total (n = 87)
1 day	100%	89%	84%	91%
1–2 days	0%	11%	16%	9%

Table 2.2 Reasons for choosing course length

Reason	LEA	GM	Independent	Total % in sample
What providers offer	28%	53%	25%	34%
Cost/time	37%	9%	16%	20%
Disruption	28%	26%	49%	36%
Miscellaneous	6%	11%	9%	9%
Total	99%	99%	99%	99%

strong, and cost (and shortage of cash) centrally imposed. Nevertheless, it should be noted that both other factors played equally quite prominent roles (28%) in this sector. The situation in the GM sector was quite different. Here, cost and time were very minor constraints (9%); as were considerations of disruption (26%). In this case, issues of what providers offered were much more prominent (53%). Again, the situation differed for the independent sector. Whilst considerations of cost and time were slight (16%), and issues of what providers offered were also not large (24%), twice as much consideration (49%) was given to questions of disruption.

It is hard to interpret any of these data as 'market driven'. The overriding importance of cost in the LEA sector suggests that because they were disadvantageously funded in this respect vis-à-vis the other two sectors, they were not competing on a level playing field with them, and nor were they able to adopt a user-driven approach which a market approach suggests. Moreover, even in the GM sector, where finance was not such a problem, actual provision offered was an overriding and inhibiting consideration; and clearly a market cannot operate where choice is not believed to be available. Finally, whilst disruption was overridingly important for the independent sector, and this was in one sense a choice based on user preference, it was an essentially negative choice, rather than one based on what was best INSET provision. What appeared to exist, then, was a market not working. This was either because the user lacked the finance to enter it or because there was perceived to be a lack of choice within it or because it was used only in a negative sense. Whichever way it is viewed, markets in INSET provision for all three sectors appeared to be ineffective.

Present INSET sector priorities

Schools were given an open-response section on the questionnaire and asked to list the major topic areas for in-service provision as identified in their school's management plan, though they were not asked to prioritise these. When priorities are referred to, then, they refer to the priorities of a school sector as a whole, rather than any one school's individual priorities.

Nevertheless, it does not seem unreasonable to suggest some degree of linkage between overall popularity of an INSET area within a school sector, and its importance to individual schools within this sector.

In terms of the number of topics and number of actual responses, across the three sectors a total of 51 discrete priority areas were identified for the current two years and a nearly comparable picture emerged for the next two. The difference between the three sectors regarding diversity of requirements was slight, despite market predictions that there should be more. This lack of diversity was replicated for the next two years, where a nearly comparable picture existed.

The frequency with which each area was indicated by schools was then totalled and a prioritised list for INSET topics by sector and for the overall sample was compiled. Percentages describe the number of times an area was chosen by all of the schools in that sector, rather than as a direct comparison with other areas of choice. The top ten areas are shown in Tables 2.3 and 2.4.

An examination of the sector priorities, as well as those of the sample as a whole, is very revealing. In all three sectors, subject/National Curriculum interests (they appear to be indissolubly linked) were the most popular choice. This perhaps should not be surprising: subject teaching is the primary means of school organisation at the secondary level in all three sectors, secondary

Table 2.3 Ranked in-service sector priorities (1992–4)

Rank	LEA maintained	Grant maintained	Independent	Overall
1	NC/subject 69%	NC/subject 71%	NC/subject 74%	NC/subject 71%
2	Management 59%	IT 46%	Pastoral care 33%	Management 38%
3	IT 45%	Management 39%	Appraisal 22%	IT 37%
4	Assessment 41%	Differentiation 36%	Ofsted 18%	Differentiation 26%
5	Differentiation 34%	SEN 32%	IT 18%	Pastoral care 24%
6	Pastoral care 24%	Assessment 25%	Management 14%	Assessment 23%
7	Teaching and learning styles 24%	Ofsted 18%	Drugs education 14%	Appraisal 19%
8	SEN 20%	Appraisal 18%	RoA 11%	SEN 18%
9	Counselling 17%	Pastoral care 14%	Counselling 11%	Ofsted 17%
10	Appraisal 17%	Counselling/GNVQ 11%	Children Act Health & Safety 11%	Counselling 13%

schools are staffed overwhelmingly by subject specialists; they are geared to the taking of subject-based examinations at the end of their pupils' period of attendance; and finally they have had to come to terms with the new discourse, requirements and organisation of the National Curriculum. This latter incorporates the vast majority of independent schools, whose pupils expect to take examinations as an entry to the job market, examinations based on the National Curriculum. Independent schools may not, like the public sector, be legally required to teach the National Curriculum, but they abstain at their competitive peril.

What are as interesting are the choices that come next. Whilst for both the LEA and GM sectors, Management and Information Technology (IT) were prioritised next, IT was rated only fifth by the independent sector, and Management was rated only sixth. However, again perhaps this is not too surprising: independent schools are long established in self-management, and consequently the introduction of the computer equipment necessary for this was very likely well in hand for some considerable time. The other two sectors, however, have had to develop strategies and competences in these areas following the legislation of the last decade, and appeared to be still going through this process.

Independent schools, by contrast, have been able to maintain their commitment to a high priority for the Pastoral Care of their pupils (placed second): a reflection, probably, of their long-established facility in Management and IT, of their genuine commitment to the personal development of their pupils, of its needed priority, particularly in boarding schools, and also of the positive effect it has for word-of-mouth marketing, initially by students, and then by their parents. Indeed, if Drugs Education (no. 7) and Counselling (no. 9) were placed within the orbit of Pastoral Care, then this area assumes an even stronger second place (58%). This is not to discount the emphasis on Pastoral Care in the other two sectors: if joined with Counselling, it would be placed fourth in the LEA sector (41%), and sixth in the GM sector (25%). None of these figures on Pastoral Care are positively or negatively indicative of market influences. A good school, it might be argued, should have a commitment to educational values as well as an eye to market demands. A strong emphasis on Pastoral Care appears to cater for both demands.

In the independent sector's list of priorities, it is also interesting to note the place of Appraisal at no. 3, which could signal its commitment to staff development. It could also indicate an awareness by it of the need to keep in line with developments in the state sector, as is evidenced by its listing of Ofsted at no. 4. All independent schools listed as members of the HMC had agreed to be given Ofsted-style inspections within the next couple of years (1994–6), a clear indication of a perceived market-driven need to be seen by the public as transparent and accountable in their dealings as the state sector. The lower rating of these two areas in the LEA sector would seem to imply that the pressure points created by them may have been passed through already.

In-service sector priorities for the next two years

Respondents were asked to indicate which areas they anticipated would inform their in-service work for the coming two years. A total of 53 priority areas were identified, about the same as for the previous two years. There were 24 new areas, though a similar number dropped out. Over the four-year period a total of 75 INSET choices were identified, with a fairly even spread of INSET topics between the three sectors. The ranked priorities for the next two years between the three sectors are shown in Table 2.4. The data in this table make interesting comparisons both between sectors and with the data presented in Table 2.3.

First, the data reflect a growing need to respond to internally and legislatively generated pressures. Thus, there was no appreciably greater diversity between the LEA, GM and the independent sectors in terms of areas chosen, suggesting that the market had not affected its 'natural' sector more than the other two. Second, there was very little change in the most popular

Table 2.4 Ranked in-service sector priorities (1995–7)

Rank	LEA maintained	Grant maintained	Independent	Overall
1	NC/subject (52%)	NC/subject (55%)	NC/subject (52%)	NC/subject (53%)
2	Management (45%)	IT (48%)	Pastoral care (28%)	IT (30%)
3	Assessment (31%)	Differentiation (26%)	Ofsted (24%)	Management (30%)
4	SEN (27%)	SEN (26%)	Management training (29%)	SEN (20%)
5	IT (24%)	Management (22%)	IT (16%)	Assessment (18%)
6	Vocational (20%)	Vocational (22%)	Appraisal (12%)	Ofsted (18%)
7	Differentiation (20%)	Ofsted (22%)	Staff development (12%)	Pastoral care (18%)
8	Teaching & learning styles (20%)	Assessment (18%)	Health & Safety (8%)	Differentiation (17%)
9	Pastoral care (20%)	Teaching and learning styles (11%)	Marketing (8%)	Vocational (15%)
10	Evaluation (13%)	Pastoral care (7%)	PSE (8%)	Teaching and learning styles (12%)

sector choices: both first and second choices in all three sectors remained the same. Finally, where there were changes, these appear to be as much the product of legislation and internal issues as of market issues. Thus, in the independent sector, the 'legislative' areas of Ofsted, Health and Safety, and National Curriculum all maintained or improved their positions. As if to offset this, marketing appears for the first time. In the LEA and GM sectors, SEN INSET (following new SEN directives in 1994) is the one area that improves in both. The evidence, then, suggests that the market is not having the effect it might.

Perceptions of sources of pressure for in-service

Further detailed information on this second hypothesis was sought from respondents concerning whether they felt their choices were driven by external pressures, internal pressures, or by a combination of both. Respondents were asked to supply this information for the previous two years and then, on a separate page, to give their prognosis for the coming two years. Their responses showing the division between external, internal, or a combination of both sources of pressures varied somewhat surprisingly. Whilst schools in the LEA sector very strongly believed in a movement towards greater internal determination of INSET provision, both the GM and the independent sectors differed very little, either between each other, or in terms of their own past and future influences. Both the GM and the independent sectors maintained that pressures were a combination of both internal and external influences. Why was there this disparity? The most likely explanation is that LEA schools were voicing a comparative judgement. Such has been the extent of external imposition over the past few years upon this sector, that any diminution in this would appear as an opportunity to exercise greater internal direction. Whilst the GM sector had faced many of the same legislative demands, schools within this sector had been granted greater self-management powers and therefore they, like their counterparts in the independent sector, had had rather greater choice of direction, and so probably saw the same amount of future external direction (as the LEA schools) as, instead, being a situation of 'no change'. Such an analysis tends to be supported by the perception of independent schools of a slight decline in their own internal control: reflecting increasing concerns with National Curriculum implementation, linked to Ofsted-style inspections, as well as concerns from Health and Safety legislation and the Children's Act. What is very clear from the data is that there was a marked degree of convergence between the three sectors, which again was not in line with free-market predictions.

School-ranked assessment of specific areas of pressure

To pursue this analysis further, schools were then asked to rank nine factors derived from the literature, each according to a six-point scale indicating strength of influence with 1 representing very strong influence and 6 very weak influence. The nine factors were:

- external legislative requirements (Leg)
- business pressures (Bus)
- parental pressures (Par)
- community concerns (Com)
- competition from other schools (Cmp)
- staff personal demand (Stf)
- school curriculum innovation (SCur)
- pupil needs (PupN)
- subject updating (Subj).

The results of the analyses of the responses to these nine criteria (Table 2.5) make it clear that for the previous two years (1992–4) and for the coming two years (1995–7) the factors that were rated as of greater influence were largely internally generated: staff personal needs, school curriculum, pupil needs and subject updating. Only in the case of legislative demands was any attention to external demands paid. The mean scores for the other external factors, competition, community pressure, parental demand and business, gave a slight indication of a little more importance in the coming two years but the variation was not great.

A key argument in favour of the market has long been the epistemic argument which suggests that it is at the individual level that decisions about transactions are best made and that central planning cannot make appropriate decisions (see Hayek 1960, Gray 1992). Over a four-year period such as was covered in this survey, it would have been reasonable to suggest that if a market was in operation there might have been clearer signs of difference

Table 2.5 Mean scores for in-service pressure factors by sector 1992–4 (L2) and 1995–7 (N2)

	LEA		Sector GM		Independent		Sample means	
Factor	L2	N2	L2	N2	L2	N2	L2	N2
Leg	2.08	2.00	1.81	2.61	3.03	2.65	2.31	2.45
Bus	4.86	4.52	4.48	4.13	4.39	4.27	4.75	4.30
Par	4.66	4.55	4.52	4.39	4.33	4.16	4.52	4.38
Com	4.23	3.85	4.52	4.21	4.04	4.12	4.28	4.07
Cmp	5.00	4.77	4.36	3.91	4.16	3.79	4.50	4.14
Stf	2.04	1.81	2.00	1.78	1.81	1.57	1.92	1.73
SCur	1.56	1.43	1.55	1.29	2.00	1.74	1.71	1.49
PupN	1.59	1.45	1.71	1.42	1.84	1.70	1.71	1.52
Subj	1.63	1.81	1.46	1.67	1.37	1.51	1.48	1.66

between the overall means for the last two years with those for the previous two. This was not indicated by the data.

Perhaps even more importantly, if a market was in operation, one would have expected to see significant differences between sectors. To determine this latter point, a one-way analysis of variance was performed on the data, to see if there were any significant differences between each of the sector types with regard to their perceptions of pressures driving INSET choices. At the 10% level, significant differences were found only in respect of legislative influence, competition and curriculum during the previous two years and for the coming two years significant differences were found only for competition and curriculum between the sectors. No significant differences, then, exist for seven of the nine factors in any of the three sectors for the coming two years. This also represents less diversity when compared to the analyses for the previous two years when there were significant differences between three of the nine factors. If the operation of a market had been developing, then it would surely be reasonable to expect that these two outcomes would be reversed. These findings, then, reinforce the argument for the weakness of market influence.

Besides the weakness of market influence, a number of further issues are also raised by the analysis. First, legislative influence was the only external factor upon choice of INSET which was rated as important by any of the sectors, and then more so by the LEA and the GM sectors, than the independent sector. This is perhaps not too surprising, given that it is these two latter sectors that have experienced legislative imposition. However, with the increased involvement in Ofsted-style inspections, increased attention to Health and Safety, implications from the Children's Act, as well as appraisal by the independent sector, one might predict that the perceived importance of such legislative influence in the independent sector will rise. Importantly, this means that a key feature of market provision – the idea of a choice of INSET determined by the school – continues to be undermined in all three sectors.

Second, and notwithstanding increased independent school perceptions of external legislative pressures, it was clear that a level playing field did not exist between the sectors: the independent sector still had to pay less attention to this area. If this was the case, it would differentially affect schools' respective abilities to plan and participate according to the needs they perceived, rather than according to those needs that derived from government legislation.

Third, whilst all three sectors rated all the internal factors more highly than any of the external factors (including legislative influence) all three sectors rated curriculum influences most highly, though the independent sector rated it slightly less so. The LEA and GM sectors had a National Curriculum imposed upon them, and therefore had had little choice but to devise implementation strategies. The independent sector still had to conform to most of its dictates; after all, examinations were and still are framed in terms of its requirements. Similarly, all three sectors, as noted above, were curriculum-driven, subject orientation forming the life-blood of all of them.

Finally, the independent sector saw and continued to see competitive influences as an important influence upon INSET choice. The GM sector had taken this view for the coming two years, but the LEA schools still discounted this as a factor in choice of provision. Thus, the sector most used to competition rated its influence highly; the sector moving into it increasingly gave it priority, whilst the sector least committed to the philosophy behind it, and most under-resourced in terms of ability to participate in it, paid it least attention. However, the underlying message was clear: the influence of the market appeared to exist strongly only with those who embraced its principles, and who had the resources to compete in it.

Conclusions

The data reported suggest that it is possible to draw conclusions regarding the three questions posed at the beginning of this chapter, namely:

- To what extent is the market determining what INSET is chosen by schools?
- Is there greater choice in provision, such as in terms of areas covered, and in terms of length of course?
- Is there equal or differential access to the market?

These are summarised below and in Table 2.6.

First, with respect to whether the market was determining INSET choice, it would seem that this was happening only partially at best. Market influences did not appear to have developed over the previous two years, nor did they appear to be determining INSET choice differentially between the three sectors. This is hardly good support for a picture of the market playing a major and active role in INSET provision.

Second, market advocates would find little support in the fact that there appeared to be no significantly greater choice in INSET provision, either in terms of course length, in terms of areas covered, or differentially between the sectors.

Third, it seems clear that LEA schools in particular felt that markets in INSET were neither effective nor fair; they believed that there were too many factors working against them to allow equal access to the market. Thus, for example with relation to the length of course, cost was between more than twice to over four times as important for LEA-sector schools as the other two sectors, indicating that schools in the LEA-maintained sector did not feel they could operate anything like as freely in a market as they might wish.[1] However, part of this inability of the LEA sector to engage equally in market competition also stemmed from inequitable continuing strong central

Table 2.6 Is the market working?

Question	Answer	Evidence
1. Is the market determining INSET choice?		
(a) Yes, no, partly	Yes	Independent sector recognises pressure of competition (p. 42)
	Partly	Independent sector taking account of Ofsted and NC (Tables 2.3 & 2.4)
	Partly	Differences for 2nd and 3rd choices (Tables 2.3 & 2.4)
	Partly	Independent and GM see internal and external driving INSET (p. 41)
	No	GM consideration of lack of choice (Table 2.2)
	No	Overall mean internal generation of pressure (Table 2.5)
	No	Legislative only major external influence (p. 43)
	No	Legislative and funding influences on INSET (Table 2.7)
(b) Increasingly?	No	No increase in topic choice (p. 40)
	No	LEA see movement to internal pressure (p. 41)
	No	Little change in internal generation overall (Table 2.5)
	No	Only three areas show any pressure differences (p. 43)
(c) Differentially between sectors?	No	No difference in number of topics chosen (p. 38)
	No	Only two out of nine areas show pressure differences (pp. 42–3)
2. Is there greater choice?		
(a) In course length?	No	Predominance of one-day course (Table 2.1)
(b) In areas covered?	No	GM consideration of lack of choice (Table 2.2)
	No	Same top priority, NC/curriculum for all sectors (Tables 2.3, 2.4)
(c) Differentially between sectors?	No	Predominance of one-day course (Table 2.1)
3. Is there equal access to the market?	No	Different pupil–teacher ratios (p. 36)
	No	Cost considerations of LEA affect course length (Table 2.2)
	No	Independent sector sees legislative influence as less than GM or LEA (p. 43)

45

Table 2.7 In-service priority areas in relation to statute/funding (state sector only)

Priority area	White Paper/Statute	Funding help
National Curriculum/ subject-related work	1988 Education Reform Act Ofsted	GEST funding
Management	Better schools Education Reform Act 1988	GEST funding
IT	Better schools	TVEI/NCET
Differentiation	Better schools Ofsted	
Assessment	Education Reform Act 1988	GEST funding
Appraisal	Circular 12/91	Appraisal funding
SEN	SEN Code of Practice	
Ofsted	1992 Education (Schools) Act	

direction in many in-service choices of the state sector, and this reason therefore also largely applies to the GM sector as well.

This central direction may be adduced from an examination of the then current INSET areas which reveal, not a market-led prioritisation, but instead a strong centrally imposed direction, which had been achieved either through the use of legislation (such as the 1988, 1992, and 1994 Education Acts) or through the injection of targeted cash (as in the Technical and Vocational Education Initiative (TVEI)). None of this, of course, is consonant with a free-market philosophy. Examples supporting this argument are summarised in Table 2.7.

Additional support for the argument that INSET in the state sector was determined much more by the influence of 'central planning' than the professed operation of the market is provided by the establishment by the DES/DfE of annual national INSET priorities and levels of funding support following Circular 6/86 (DES 1986).

It is important to note here that whichever way one interprets these data, they signify a distortion of policy based on the philosophy of the market-place. If the independent sector is disadvantaged by exclusion from such earmarked financial provision for INSET in the LEA and GM sectors, as intimated in Table 2.7, then the operation of the market is distorted in favour of the state sectors. If this is merely the same amount of 'per pupil' funding/money but with a percentage ring-fenced and centrally directed by government for in-service, then it still distorts market-based provision because it imposes, in the state sectors, central direction upon what should be a market-determined operation. However, this is no simple description of convergence between school sectors. It seems clear that whilst there are areas of convergence, there are areas of continued dissimilarity. Thus, there appear to be three kinds of convergence between the sectors.

1   There are areas of legislation that all are having to follow, willy-nilly: these would include aspects of the National Curriculum, Assessment, Ofsted-style inspections, the Health and Safety legislation, and the Children's Act.
2   Style of funding is now similarly determined by means of pupil numbers.
3   There are internal managerial issues, which have been extensively borrowed from business and industry, and which all three sectors are adopting. These would include appraisal, performance indicators, and quality assurance procedures.

However, even if there are clear areas of convergence – which militate against the plurality of market provision – there are also areas of continuing dissimilarity. These would include:

• the ability of the independent sector to specify and vary the price placed on each child;
• the ability of the independent sector to select between aspects of legislation, all of which may be mandatory for the state sector;
• the different pupil/teacher ratios;
• the ability of a school/sector to afford specific kinds of INSET.

All of these aspects, whilst preserving dissimilarity, do not encourage a true market, as they effectively disadvantage the state sector, and LEA schools in particular.

Two final points may be made here. The first is, as noted above, that whilst the results show a mixed or poor effect of market influences on INSET provision, this does not begin to address the question of whether the market should play a significant role in INSET provision. It is at least debatable how far the market should intrude into the determination of what schools provide. Grace (1994), for example, argues that whilst it is partly an empirical matter as to whether market provision would provide individuals with more information and participation in their local services, considerations of its viability must go beyond this, for the nature of the service can induce a concern for merely private good and individual return, or a wider conception of social and political responsibilities. Bridges in Bridges and McLaughlin (1994) makes a similar point when he distinguishes between positional and non-positional goods. Positional goods benefit individual students and schools, but not the wider population of a country; non-positional benefits confer benefits not only to individuals and institutions, but also to a population at large, and are, he believes, the hallmark of an educated culture. The difference, he suggests, lies in the effect they have on people:

> the more a system of schooling offers the opportunity ... to secure positional advantage, the more [parents] will (quite rationally) exercise their custodial responsibility to secure that advantage for their children and the less they will concern themselves with ensuring that the system provides non-positional benefits to all. (p. 77)

The result, he suggests, is almost inevitable:

> The richer, educative and universally beneficial purposes of schooling will become subordinate to the narrower, self-interested function which can benefit some only at the expense of others. (ibid.)

The same can clearly apply to INSET policy. If INSET is directed solely by school self-interest in a market, it will probably fail to address questions that transcend parochial, sectional, or temporally limited concerns, and will almost certainly have long-term damage upon teachers' professionalism. In the long run, this cannot be good for a country's education or societal well-being. The point then is this: markets may not be delivering in the manner or to the degree apparently supported by Conservative governments over the last fifteen years, and still apparently by the present Labour Government, but this need not be a particularly bad thing, and can only be decided by further (philosophical) arguments about the nature and extent of 'public goods', which will be developed during the remainder of this book.

Finally, if one model, that of the free market, does not fit too well the provision of INSET investigated, is there a model, or models, that fit better? At least three issues need to be considered here:

1   the heavy emphasis of schools INSET upon internal matters;
2   the heavy emphasis within the state sector upon external, legislative imposition and direction, and the increased interest in this area by the independent sector;
3   despite the lack of market impact upon INSET provision, the continued use by successive governments of markets to 'ginger up' school performance.

The first of these, an interest in internal matters, is probably a reflection not only of the natural inclination of any organisation to pay attention to matters that affect its internal day-to-day running, but also of a more distinctive and long-standing cultural tradition in schools to concentrate upon internal 'professional matters' (Grace 1995). Even the heaviest market and legislative pressure will probably not divert interest from some aspects of internal running, though it should probably cause less time to be spent on them in the long run. However, even granting this, the strong legislative influence and continued governmental use of markets suggest that another force is at work which may not be that of a real market, but of a centrally laid-down policy which encourages schools to compete only at the level of implementation.

The rationale for this is perhaps best summed up in terms of a post-Fordist rather than a free-market model. It is a phenomenon that can be seen on a much wider stage than education (Burrows and Loader 1994, Gilbert *et al.* 1992), as societies' economic structures, predicated upon assembly lines, mass production and mass consumption, with strong centralist direction mediated by many layers of managers, come to be replaced by competing smaller units, less managerial layers, and greater devolved responsibility, but the same degree of centralist control mediated by an explosion in microtechnology. Nevertheless, it has its applications to education (see Smyth 1993, Bottery 1994), and fits the INSET scenario described above rather well; one in which free-market exhortations are constrained by continued – or increasing – centralist imposition, and in which responsibility is located at the periphery, whilst power remains at the centre.[2]

The final conclusion of this chapter, then, is that three agendas appear to be working side by side in INSET provision, and begin to suggest a particular model which teachers are being directed into practising. The three agendas in INSET provision stem, it seems, partly from issues internal to school functioning, partly from market exhortations, but most influentially from post-Fordist constraints. If this is the case, then it seems fair to conclude that the market is not so much working in INSET, as acting as a cover for a centralist agenda. Crucially, it indicates that a post-Fordist model of teacher professionalism is being suggested; one that demands of the teaching profession no deep and extended commitment to an overview of education, but one concerned primarily with devising strategies for the implementation of policy created elsewhere. What is probably even more worrying is that if this model is being offered, there is evidence to suggest that the teaching profession may have already begun to accept it. These themes – centralisation of policy and teacher complicity – are the subject of the next two chapters.

3

TEACHERS' PROFESSIONAL DEVELOPMENT

The need for an appreciation of the public and ecological natures of their work

We can get bogged down in academics – what we really want is time to implement the National Curriculum.

(Comment by headteacher)

Introduction

The previous chapters have established that right-wing ideas have had a significant impact on governments and educational institutions in many countries. Indeed, in many ways they still set the agenda for the management and administration of these educational systems. Concerns over bureaucratic inefficiencies, producer quality, greater customer responsiveness and choice are all normally perceived to have been driven by radical liberal thought over the last two decades, and continue to be a dominant strain of New Modernist thought.

These influences, as we have seen, have had a long history and stem from philosophical, political, economic, and ethical concerns, as well as from the more pragmatic belief that most of the educational systems of the Western industrialised nations have been 'failing' their countries over the last couple of decades at least. From such beliefs, then, have stemmed system-wide reforms which, their proponents claimed, have attempted – among other things – to provide greater power to the consumer, greater responsiveness by the provider, and ultimately, it is argued, produce better quality, efficiency and effectiveness in educational provision.

These claims are evaluated in detail elsewhere (Whitty *et al.* 1998, Bridges and McLaughlin 1994, LeGrand and Bartlett 1993, Bottery 1992, Hindess (ed.) 1990). The purpose of this chapter is, in part, to contribute to that debate, but it is more centrally concerned with pointing out that such reforms have highlighted and exacerbated a problem that has existed for some considerable time. This is that the teaching profession spends too little time thinking about issues that ask fundamental questions about the purposes of an education system – and therefore of a teaching profession – within a particular kind of society. It will be argued that a well-articulated defence of teachers' professionalism is possible only when teachers are aware of the 'public' context of their teaching, and of the historical, political and sociological reasons for the current nature of their practice.

This chapter will begin by sketching the parameters of this issue by examining notions of reflection, and what professionals need to reflect upon, before proceeding to assess findings in this area which includes the research conducted by the authors. It will conclude by indicating the lack of attention paid to the issues raised, as well as considering the necessary remediation.

Reflection and the provision of continuing professional development

The in-service education and continuing professional development (CPD) of teachers must not only contain a grounding in the latest knowledge and skills that they or others feel are necessary for executing the latest ideas for classroom practice. Whilst this is necessary, it is not sufficient. Space must be provided within CPD for professions to reflect upon current practice, and how they conceive doing their job. The notion of reflection is currently one of the more fashionable phrases within professional development literature at the present time, and particularly that of 'reflective practice'. Its insights – and problems – provide a useful starting point for this chapter.

The term 'reflective practice' stems primarily from the writings of Donald Schön (1983, 1987), and basically suggests that there are at least three levels of professional practice. The first is that of 'technical rationality'. This is the level at which a problem presents itself, the professional searches through his or her bank of expertise, and then selects the appropriate solution and applies it. Schön suggests that Western society in general has become wedded to a conception of such technical expertise. This is partly because of a still thriving acceptance of Enlightenment ideas of scientific 'objectivity', partly because of the opportunities presented to professional bodies for prestige and financial gain from the adoption of such an approach, and partly because of the general public's desire to have experts who know the answers. Yet one might characterise the intellectual temper of this century by the gradual erosion of such belief. This is in part because of the experience of two world wars unparalleled in their destructive capacity and the extent to which scientific findings were drawn upon to increase the killing rate; because of global disasters which have contributed to, or were undiminished by, scientific practices; by instances of malpractice in all the major professions; and through an increasingly sceptical philosophical and professional literature surrounding the whole notion of objectivity – as evidenced in the current plethora of 'post-modernist' writings. 'Technical rationality' then serves only those who would do the directing of such technical rationalists; on its own it is a blind, unreflective and dangerous animal. It cannot be the model for professional practice.

The next of Schön's levels of practice is that of 'thinking like a ...'. This is where the novice is not only trained in the technical expertise of that profession, but is also inducted into its habits and expectations, so that actions are performed in the spirit of the profession, without being specifically tied to individual situations. Whilst such an approach is more flexible than that of 'technical rationality', it still suffers from the problem of stemming from only one value viewpoint, whether this be a professional viewpoint or any other. Indeed, one dominant theme running through philosophical and political theory over the past three decades has been the awareness that pronouncements on issues reflect a particular view of the world, and almost certainly a view generated by, and supportive of, a particular position of power. The activities of professions are now cited as good examples of this. It is an insightful task to trace the evolution of literature on the professionals, from a tradition early in the century which concentrated almost exclusively upon hagiographies of individual great professionals, through to an analysis of the term 'professional', which tended to focus upon concepts of expertise, altruism, and trust, to a present awareness and concern with issues of power. Collins (1990, p. 26), for instance, describes professional activities primarily in terms of 'market closure', and that:

> instead of merely responding to market dynamics ... occupations attempt to control market conditions. Some occupations are relatively successful at this, others less so. Those which are especially successful are the ones which we have come to call the professions.

Now it may be thought that both 'technical rationality' and 'thinking like a ...' are techniques that need not be contaminated by such macro-social issues as professional power. Attempting to find effective ways of devising and implementing a History curriculum, for example, may seem a long way from such debates, and would seem to involve a considerable amount of, but nothing more than, hard work at these first two levels. And that, it might be argued, means that most – even all – of the core of professional practice can be encapsulated within these two levels. The research presented in this chapter suggests this is a view held by many in the teaching profession today.

Yet if one allies questions of what selection of knowledge will be incorporated into a curriculum, to questions about which particular slant will be adopted in its dissemination and evaluation, then it should be clear that such issues cannot and must not be divorced from their social and political context. Indeed, one might argue that this is particularly so for teachers if they have limited control over what goes into the curriculum, or of the forms of assessment that may drive its selection. This is a situation that accurately describes the education systems of many countries, and which is exacerbated in organisations where senior management teams provide little or no provision of CPD in such discussions.

Schön is therefore probably correct when he suggests that the first problem for a professional is in deciding what the issue or problem is, part of which will be by reference to this wider context. Without grounding such issues within their macro-social contexts, teachers may end up applying merely 'technical rational' solutions, derived from bodies of 'knowledge' which cannot claim to be objective in either their selection or purposes.

However, Schön does not provide all the answers. His description of professional practice falls some way short of the picture we wish to paint. He is undoubtedly correct in suggesting that because each situation is unique, and yet each has points of similarity, there must be an intuitive element as professionals 'play' with different schemes and different approaches in their attempts to see which best 'fits' the problem. This must mean that a professional, in order better to understand the question at hand, should consult different interested parties in order to gain their understanding and 'framing' of the issue. It should be noted that this means that consultation by professionals of significant stakeholders then ceases to be a strategy devised merely as a response to consumer 'free-market' pressure – as indeed some of the quality literature also suggests (see Crosby 1979, Bottery 1994) – but instead becomes embedded within a conception of professional practice as requiring other perspectives for its better prosecution. This is an important point which will build into the picture of professional practice that this book will propose.

The public/private divide

Schön's work may also be criticised for concentrating upon 'artistic' professionals, and illegitimately generalising from their experience to others. There seems some truth in this, but there is also another – and from the perspective of this book – more important dimension to professional practice which he fails to take into account. This we shall call the 'public/private' dimension. Thus, probably because Schön concentrates exclusively upon professionals who are either self-employed, or who operate for companies in the private sector, such as architects, psychoanalysts, counsellors, and musicians, he fails to take into account a dimension of professional practice perhaps better highlighted when one considers the work of public-sector professionals like doctors, police, social workers, and teachers. These, it might be argued, have an extra commitment to a notion of 'public good', to the development and health of their communities, and to expanded notions of citizenship: values that are not so strongly demanded of their private counterparts. So it might be argued that whilst these private-sector professionals may voluntarily commit themselves to developing these values, in actuality they need concern themselves with little more than the viability of their organisation, and the quality of their practice. It is certainly implicit within the role of public-sector professionals that they need to consider the nature of their role not only within an organisation, but within a societal context as well, precisely because the public domain is a necessary focus for the promotion of collective life, as opposed to the prosecution of individual interests. Thus Ranson and Stewart (1989) argue that the private and public institutions differ from each other in terms of the nature of their work, because (p. 5) 'a concept of organisation that encompasses citizens differs from an organisation that knows only customers'.

Similarly, Grace (1989) suggests that the marketised approach to education seen in the business sector necessarily encourages the pursuit of individualistic, selfish motives, precisely because this is what a market is set up to do (with, of course, the belief that it will lead to a better outcome overall). Such an approach, then, cannot appreciate that there are some areas of human activity that need to be seen as public goods, and not merely as private activities. A public good, on the other hand, is one where a society acknowledges the need for provision of a service for all, even for those who cannot afford it, because its provision is seen as essential for the well-being of that society as a whole. As Grace (p. 214) argues:

> Might not education be regarded as a public good because it seeks to develop in all citizens a moral sense, a sense of social and fraternal responsibility for others and a disposition to act in rational and co-operative ways? The ultimate foundation for democracy ... and for a truly participative and intelligent political process ... depends upon the education of its people and the extent to which they can articulate and feel confident about the rights of citizenship. Insofar as education provides the basic conditions for making democracy possible it has an immediate claim to the status of being a public good.

But is this strictly true of all private-sector organisations? It certainly can (and has) been argued that individuals working within private-sector organisations, driven by the logic of the market, and by the demands of a competitive situation, have their minds focused upon institutional rather than public contexts, and come to conceptualise their jobs within a context of institutional survival (Bottery 1998). Yet to this picture need to be added a number of other complicating factors.

First, it seems highly likely that despite the constraints of a market situation, public goods can still be a focus for private organisations. Charities fit this description precisely, and English independent schools are, in the vast majority of cases, registered charities, organisations that, by definition, could be seen engaging in activities that benefit the community. Further, such registration for charitable status requires that they be non-profit making in a commercial sense, and any surplus made has to be put back into the charity by its trustees. In this respect their situation is not wildly dissimilar to that in the UK of maintained schools operating under

LMS (Local Management of Schools) where any surplus on the accounts for any financial year has to be put back into the school and carried over into the next year.

Indeed, it could be argued that a key part of the vision of some private schools for their existence may be as much to do with contributing to a 'public good', as it is for institutions in the state sector – whatever advocates of state education may feel about the inequalities of the state/private school divide. Thus, many independent schools stress a commitment of service to the community at large with emphasis on programmes like the Duke of Edinburgh Award scheme and the Combined Cadet Force (CCF). The following quotes taken from private-school prospectuses in England illustrate this point:

> The Sixth Form runs the District Talking Newspaper for the Blind, while others work at local schools, with the elderly, with the handicapped or on conservation projects.

> There are opportunities for Sixth Formers to take part in community service work ... including helping in hospital wards or local primary schools.

> We aim to prepare our pupils ... for a full, active and responsible role in the community.

> All boys in the school are encouraged to commit themselves to the welfare of those less fortunate. ... the school has close contacts with local homes, hospitals and charitable organisations.

So, in the light of these three reasons – the legal implications and requirements of charitable status, the comments of the Goodman Report (1976) and the evidence from the sample – there seem good grounds for asserting that part of the vision of some independent schools is their contribution to the provision of a 'public good', and that therefore private schools need to be as concerned about their staff's appreciation of the 'public' dimension of teaching as those schools in the state sector.

Yet, it must be stressed that since independent schools have to exist within a competitive market situation, their ability to focus upon – and to deliver – such 'public goods' will be limited, for the broader extra-curricular activities listed earlier are increasingly seen to offer a competitive advantage. For state schools, as they or any other public-sector organisations move into quasi-market situations, their ability to focus upon and deliver such 'goods' may be curtailed through, on the one hand, tighter cash limits and on the other, increasing central direction of educational agendas along functional and implementational lines. (See Clarke and Newman 1996.)

The ecology of a profession

If this is the case, then it follows that not only do teachers in both the state and the independent sectors of education find their ability to respond to 'public' values constrained by the imperatives of the market; they both need to be concerned with notions of 'public good', a promotion of the life of the community and society at large, rather than just being interested in the promotion of their organisation or personal interests. It then follows that teachers in both sectors will need to be concerned with what happens in society at large, and how these forces impact upon their practice. This is an interest in what we shall call a wider 'occupational ecology', for the manner in which this impacts upon the profession has crucial implications not only for the profession itself, but for the welfare of society as a whole.

There are a number of strong examples of this requirement for an 'ecological' perspective. Firstly, take international debates about curricular content. The introduction of National Curricula need to be located by teaching professions within a wider context of arguments for and against the conception of a national curriculum, and this needed to be debated by whole school staffs, not just by politicians and their advisers, individuals taking masters degrees at universities, or by academics in educational journals. Similarly, professionals need to move beyond the understanding of their own areas of expertise and appreciate a subject's role within an overall conception of a curriculum. Yet so often they appear to be locked into what Hargreaves (1994) calls curricular 'balkanisation' – defending their territory and their finance against other curriculum power-bases. This is a situation that limits their ability to engage with a bigger picture, one that suggests that the way in which subjects are prioritised has societal implications, as preferences indicate, and help to create, different kinds of (challengeable) priorities and values within society as a whole. Further, any exhortations to teaching professions to engage in more disseminatory practice reminds one that choice of teaching style is more than a case of personal preference, but has implications for the creation of the kind of adults one may wish to see in the future. Descriptions of the reasons for the adoption of teaching styles in the early development of organised education in the Western world certainly bear this out:

> Mass education was the ingenious machine constructed by industrialism to produce the kind of adults it needed ... the solution was an educational system that, in its very structure, stimulated this new world ... the most criticised features of education today – the regimentation, lack of individualisation, the rigid system of seating, grouping, grading and marking, the authoritarian style of the teacher – are precisely those that made mass public education so effective an instrument of adaptation for its time and place ... the child did not simply learn facts that he could use later on: he lived, as well as

learned, a way of life modelled after the one he would lead in the future.

(Toffler 1970, pp. 354–5)

Finally, the situation that schools face in terms of market demands, needs to be placed within a wider conception than that of simply working out the best means of attracting new students. Professional development courses need to be couched initially in such questions as:

- Is competition the best way of running an educational system?
- Are internal markets the same as ordinary markets?
- Are other professions facing similar market-led changes?
- Are pupils and parents merely customers, or something more and different?
- Does the use of industrial analogies affect the way teachers think and speak? Is this helpful or unhelpful?
- How can we obviate any excesses of a market situation?

Such issues, then, suggest that professionals in both the public and private sectors need to incorporate a high degree of reflection into their consultation with interested parties, and must also have an acute understanding of the political, social and ethical implications of the impact of their practice, and of changes to it. In particular, built into both teacher training and in-service education must be a 'public' conception of practice, and secondly a developing appreciation of the 'ecology' of the profession of teaching. To what extent, then, are these concerns reflected in the provision of teachers' in-service? It is to this we now turn.

Data sample and findings

There is an increasing body of international literature that suggests that governmental legislation is constraining and affecting the practice of professionals. A wide-screen perspective is given by Whitty et al. (1998), and by Graham (1998). Nationally, it can be seen in Australia in the work of Taylor et al. (1997) and Smyth (1995); in Canada by Hargreaves (1994), and by Levin and Riffel (1997). Our own study is from both the secondary and primary phases of a sample of schools from four different local education authorities in the north and east of England. The schools' in-service training or staff development officers were invited to complete a questionnaire on their schools' in-service priorities, coupled with the invitation to send us further information if they so wished. Overall 40 questionnaires were sent to secondary schools and 48 to primaries, followed by a phone call or fax after a couple of weeks from the date of the first enquiry. We received a 72.5% return from secondary schools and a return of 70.8% from primary schools.

These in-service co-ordinators were invited to describe their school's priorities for in-service provision as identified in their school management plan during the last two years (1992–4); then what they envisaged would be their priorities in the coming two years (1995–7); and finally what they would like to have as major in-service priorities in an ideal world. In smaller primary schools, the individual in charge of the provision of in-service usually turned out to be the headteacher. In their replies, these co-ordinators were able to list as many or as few priorities as were identified in their management plans. These were then collated by topic area. The responses for the secondary schools are shown in Table 3.1 and for the primaries in Table 3.2. The topics have been ranked in order of popularity.

In-service data – secondary schools

The data shown from the secondary schools, Table 3.1, indicate that there is a consistently high degree of emphasis on management throughout. One might be tempted to ask whether this emphasis should have declined, given that management has been a major priority for over a decade. More likely is that these data confirm the suggestions by Clarke and Newman (1996) that public-sector organisations are increasingly characterised by a 'managerialist' ethos because of demands for economy, efficiency, and effectiveness, a managerialism pre-occupied with the 'how to do it' or 'square the circle' syndrome, rather than a concern with overarching issues. By its very nature it is unlikely to develop an appreciation by teachers of the ecology of, or the public nature of, the profession of teaching.

A further point to note in the secondary data was the emergence of issues to do with the implementation of changes to the National Curriculum, due to the Dearing report (1994), at the top of the priorities for the ensuing two years. This may not have been much of a surprise, but it did consume a great deal of school in-service budgets and time, and given that the implementation of the new orders for the National Curriculum was a statutory requirement, again any opportunity for appreciation of the public ecology of the profession was probably squeezed out or marginalised.

The one point in Table 3.1 that might suggest a grappling with 'ecological' or 'public' professional issues was the emergence of 'evaluation' as a priority in the top ten list. If this was genuine evaluation then these larger questions might arise on a course programme. The 'ideal world' listing seems to indicate a high degree of socialisation into the present directed patterns as classroom-based work and management top the list. Interestingly areas of personal development emerge – often described as the outcomes of appraisal. One has to ask why these were all described as personal development by our respondents rather than as professional development. Whilst it might seem uncharitable to suggest that this is because many teachers have a limited understanding of what being a professional entails, other research supports

Table 3.1 In-service priorities identified by secondary staff development officers
(*n* = 29)

Ranking	Key areas during the last two years (% of schools indicating)	Likely priorities for the next two years (% of schools indicating)	Priorities in an ideal world (% of schools indicating)
1	Management (59%)	National Curriculum post Dearing (52%)	Classroom-based work (76%)
2	Information technology (45%)	Management (45%)	Management (48%)
3	Assessment (41%)	Assessment (31%)	Personal development (38%)
4	Subject-related work (38%)	SEN (27%)	Information technology (6%)
5	Differentiation (34%)	Information technology (24%)	
6	National Curriculum (31%)	Vocational education (20%)	
7	Teaching & learning styles (24%)	Differentiation (20%)	
8	Pastoral care (24%)	Teaching & learning styles (20%)	
9	SEN (20%)	Pastoral care (20%)	
10	Counselling (17%)	Evaluation (13%)	

this hypothesis. Work in the UK (Bottery 1998), and in Canada (Levin and Riffel 1997), for instance, both suggest that the majority of classroom practitioners have little grasp of, or time for an interest in, the wider issues of a public ecology which affect their practice.

Table 3.2 In-service priorities identified by primary staff development officers (*n* = 34)

Ranking	Key areas during the last two years (% of schools indicating)	Likely priorities for the next two (% of schools indicating)	Priorities in an ideal world (% of schools indicating)
1	National Curriculum work (79%)	National Curriculum work (91%)	National Curriculum work (48%)
2	Special educational needs (27%)	SENs (24%)	Staff development (45%)
3	Other subject areas (21%)	Management (15%)	Other subject areas (7%)
4 =	Assessment, IT (18%)	= Ofsted, IT (11%)	= Management, class man., SEN
6	Staff development (12%)	= Staff development, other subject areas (9%)	Differentiation, LMS, assessment, IT
7 =	Class man. Ofsted (12%)		Teaching and learning styles (3%)
8 =		Differentiation assessment (6%)	
9	Differentiation (6%)		No reply = 5
10 =	Management LMS appraisal (3%)	Class management appraisal (3%)	

In-service content data – primary

As with the secondary data, work at the primary level on areas of the National Curriculum dominated every other aspect of work, though it did drop dramatically by almost half when considerations of the provision of in-service over the next two years were compared with priorities in an ideal world. Interestingly, management issues received much less attention at this level than they did at the secondary. Perhaps the most dramatic rise, though, was in the interest shown in 'Staff Development'. This area was used to include any areas that emphasised the personal, self-chosen path of development, as opposed to the path geared solely to external or school-centred demands. As one can see, this had been held as a priority by only 12% in the previous two years, and would decline to 9% in the next two. Yet, given an ideal world, this would jump to a highly impressive 45% of time for professional development. This seems to confirm quite strongly that the kind of individualistic culture many believe primary schools to have held in the recent past was still there in spirit. National Curricular impositions have, however, strengthened subject-dominated culture. Yet while demands for collegial, team-centred approaches may have increasingly dominated approaches to in-service, they had not yet, it seems, destroyed the individualist approach to the job. It should be noted, however, that since this research the introduction of collegial team-based approaches at the primary level, particularly through the Literacy and Numeracy hours, and through the exigencies of continued Ofsted inspections, suggest that this is increasingly a rearguard action which it will be hard to sustain.

Again, as with the secondary data, there was very little here to suggest that any of the provision of in-service in any of the three categories actively engaged the teacher in either the public or ecological natures of their job (and the demands that stem from these). Whilst something to develop such concerns may have appeared within the areas of 'personal development', 'management', or 'curriculum work', there seems no necessary connection. A first main conclusion must therefore be that the provision of in-service did not in any significant way address the twin issues of such importance for the professional development of the teaching profession. This should be a major cause for concern.

Length of courses

The respondents were asked to indicate the average length of courses that their staff attended. Both primary and secondary replies showed quite emphatically that the one-day short course was the norm, though the schools did avail themselves of courses considerably longer, e.g. the primary 20-day science/maths co-ordinators courses. However, it must be noted that funding for these did not come from school budgets. Schools were also asked why they opted for that particular length of course. Responses in Table 3.3 indicate clearly that there were three main reasons:

- this was the length of course offered by providers;
- the cost and time constraints for the schools involved;
- this was the length of course that fitted current professional development needs.

Another interesting finding was the percentage of schools that recorded that they chose in-service because this was the length offered by providers. This

Table 3.3 Reasons for length of course

Reason	Primary n = 34	Secondary n = 29
What the providers offer	45%	32%
Cost & time constraints	40%	68%
Fitting professional development needs	15%	0%

was the most important reason for many primary schools, and perhaps not too surprising in a school with a small staff. Evaluating different providers, and negotiating with them over venue and cost are time-consuming tasks which can be avoided by using the services of the local authority. Nevertheless, for a school to reply that this length was chosen because this was what providers offered, suggests no input by schools. Yet one must at least hope that providers listened to their clients sufficiently so that they offered the length of courses that schools would and could pay for. It would clearly be pointless to offer week-long courses if there were no takers, and if clients indicated that cost is a key factor. Yet, a one-day course seriously restricts the possibilities of what a provider can offer; it curtails even those benefits that accrued from residential courses where much exchange and cross-fertilisation of ideas took place. As one reply put it: 'Most one-day courses are a waste of time. They entertain, they can cause some thought, but they are quickly forgotten.'

Respondents also showed that their thinking on in-service provision was governed by practical considerations far more than by curricular ones. Few respondents alluded to the content of a course affecting its length or likely choice by colleagues. This served to reinforce the very significant way in which changes in the provision of in-service, funding and school management had impinged on the socialisation of teachers and their expectations of what their professional development should consist.

Internally or externally driven?

This situation, introduced by successive changes in government policy, had and continues to have a very significant effect on the teaching profession. Respondents were asked to indicate to what extent they thought that recent in-service priorities had been driven by external legislative demand or through internally generated issues. They were then asked to indicate which of these they anticipated would be the main driving force for in-service in the next two years. Table 3.4 summarises their responses.

These data were at first sight quite surprising. It was striking that only 14% of secondary and 23% of primary schools reported that recent priorities had been driven exclusively by external demands. Whilst it could be argued that

Table 3.4 Influences generating in-service areas: staff development officers' views (secondary *n* = 29; primary *n* = 34)

	Recent priorities		New priorities	
	Secondary	Primary	Secondary	Primary
External legislation	4 (14%)	8 (24%)	4 (14%)	5 (15%)
Internally generated	7 (24%)	10 (29%)	17 (59%)	8 (23%)
Both	16 (55%)	16 (47%)	8 (27%)	21 (62%)
No reply	2 (7%)	0	0	0

schools had to follow government priorities in order to achieve funding, one would expect a higher percentage of respondents to indicate that external legislation was a major influence if they felt forced. However, when it is noted that 55% of secondary schools and 47% of primary schools believed that both internal and external demands were involved in the determination of recent priorities, it is very possible to interpret this as indicating that there had been a fusing together in the minds of schools of their priorities with those external ones of government. Put another way, it could be seen as a mark of success of government policy that their aims and priorities had been significantly taken on by schools in this respect. It may then be the case that schools had absorbed external demands so much that they had then become part of the warp and woof of day-to-day thinking. If this was the case, their selection of professional development priorities would be seen as non-controversial. This hypothesis is supported in two ways. It is supported firstly by the fact that new priorities are largely seen as internally generated. Yet this is in conflict with the data in the 'New priorities' section of Tables 3.1 and 3.2, where post-Dearing National Curriculum topped the priorities. It is supported by the lack of agreement in Tables 3.1 and 3.2 between the schools' priorities in an ideal world, and those of the other two columns. Had there been this much internal driving of in-service, one might have expected a much higher measure of agreement.

An interesting divergence between the primary and secondary data exists in that the secondary data indicated quite clearly a movement in the belief by schools that in-service had moved from a mixed position of generation, to one of much greater internal generation. Some secondary respondents indicated that the five-year moratorium on change consequent upon the Dearing Report on the National Curriculum was a prime reason for expecting future issues to be internally generated. The contradiction might be explained by arguing that much would be based around what schools would opt to do with the curriculum time 'freed' by Dearing (see Wright 1994) and this is perceived as internal.

The primary data, on the other hand, suggest a different story. The data imply that the majority of primary schools believed that the provision of professional development education in the recent past had largely been driven by both external and internal demands, though there was a significant minority of schools that believed that either external or internal influence had predominated. Now, it would appear, there was an even more firmly held belief in the need to embrace the demands of both. Thus the percentage of schools that believed that professional development education was driven by both rises from 47% for most recent in-service to 62% for the newer provision, an increase that draws equally from both 'internal' and 'external' camps. The recent primary legislation mentioned above – that on literacy and numeracy – only reinforces the external generation of in-service in this sector.

Yet an initial conclusion must be that at a time in educational history when there had been an unprecedented degree of central government involvement in policy, curriculum, management, resourcing, assessing, inspection, governance and initial and in-service provision, it is remarkable how many schools still believed that their priorities had been generated internally, or would be, or by a seemingly benign combination of internal and external. But nowhere, again, were issues of the public nature of the profession, nor of its professional ecology, asserted as of particular interest or significance.

Discussion of data

The findings from the research appear, then, to indicate three things:

- that INSET content selected by schools failed in any significant way to deal with the wider issues crucial to the development of teaching as a profession;
- that the length of courses that schools selected and were provided with added to a climate of short-termism and quick fixes;
- that schools appeared to believe that they were increasingly moving to a position where they could determine development internally, or, at the very least, where external and internal demands could be balanced.

Nevertheless, even in an 'ideal world' situation, the evidence suggests that schools would fail to address directly issues of the kind of professional nature outlined earlier. Certainly, it is possible – perhaps even probable – that discussion of the kinds of 'ecological' and 'public' issues advocated in this book did and still do take place in schools, not only on days reserved for professional development but during the normal working day, and would therefore have some impact upon school decision-making. However, because provision for professional development is heavily oriented in directions other than towards these issues, such discussion is likely to be reactive, parenthetical to issues of implementation or simply a matter of chance, rather than being, as it should be, proactive and the central focus for in-service education. It seems then, that the teaching profession in England and Wales may have left itself dangerously exposed to policy dictation from outside.

A strong conclusion must be that if government policies were seeking to change professional development education into little more than training, and thereby bring about a resultant change in the socialisation of teachers, this research indicates that they are succeeding. The data appear to indicate that government policies have exacerbated a trend evident for too long in school professional development education: an inability or unwillingness by the teaching profession to set aside sufficient time to consider actively the nature and role of the teaching profession in society. By failing to do so, they render themselves increasingly incapable of setting agendas at the macro-level, and of leaving these for others to complete. Whether they like it or not, the data indicate that teachers are being deprofessionalised, and that they consciously or unconsciously are co-operating in this deprofessionalisation.

Towards remediation

Whilst more will be said at the end of this book concerning remediation, some points need to be made here. To begin with, teachers, in order to defend themselves better, need to understand themselves better. To do this they need to do more than pay lip service to a proactive policy in this regard. Any school that says of the following three recommendations 'we talk about these things all the time', without assigning specific professional development education for their consideration and deliberation, is in reality not giving its teachers the time nor the breathing space to reflect upon them, and consequently cannot expect the level of concentration and seriousness attached to them which they merit and need. Three initial recommendations are:

- that all teachers be acquainted with and be able to debate implications for the teaching profession of the conscious adoption of the concept of the 'reflective' practitioner. This is likely to raise many kinds of questions about epistemological objectivity, the framing of problems and solutions, and the role of stakeholders in the educational process;
- that teachers acquire a greater awareness and understanding of the nature of the public/private debate. In an era when there is a continued blending of public and private-sector provision through a policy of allowing any provider to bid for provision of service so long as they can meet pre-specified quality criteria and can achieve previously designated targets, an appreciation of the different demands of these two sectors is increasingly urgent;
- that teachers acquire a greater understanding of themselves *vis-à-vis* the society in which they live. This involves asking such questions as:
  - Are inheritances from the original reasons for organised education questioned within in-service provision? An awareness of such

inheritances will enable teachers – and other professionals – more readily to understand other interested parties' reactions to that practice, and to debate with them.

–   Which aspects of the teaching profession's current practice, which it claims should be performed by credentialled individuals alone, are genuinely justified by expertise or in reality by tradition and historical accident?

–   What are the primary motivations of the teachers' representative bodies *vis-à-vis* legislation?

–   In what major respects is the teachers' situation different from or the same as other occupational groups in the public sector?

–   How does the situation of the teaching profession in this country differ from that in other countries? Why does it differ?

Such questions, moreover, need to be set within a structured and rewarded framework, which becomes as much part of the accepted agenda for professional development education as, for instance, is curriculum implementation. A half-day session will do nothing to change things. The issues raised here have been so neglected at the in-service level that they need the help of cumulative and sustained courses of education. If teachers and schools continue to lower their heads to pull their classroom or management carts, it should come as no surprise that they end up at destinations they did not select – a simple but accurate description of deprofessionalisation.

Conclusion

This chapter, then, has sought to establish whether schools have devoted enough of their professional development education time to the 'public' and 'ecological' areas of in-service education. The evidence strongly suggests that they have not, and a number of arguments have been made to suggest that this is a dangerous situation for a teaching profession to allow to happen.

However, the discussion cannot rest quite there. Whilst it has been argued that there is good evidence to suggest that teachers contribute towards their own deprofessionalisation, the data presented in this chapter could still be interpreted as suggesting that the origins of these deprofessionalised attitudes in England and Wales are to be found in legislative direction, not in teaching culture *per se*. If this was the case, then loosening up this legislative steering would essentially solve the problem. How is this to be determined? One way is to look at other sectors of schooling – such as the grant-maintained and private sectors of education – to see whether the increasing degrees of managerial and curricular freedom found in these sectors reflect a greater interest in the public and ecological dimensions than that found in the LEA sector. If these aspects do receive more attention here, this would add strong support to the argument that it is very largely central direction that is the cause of the problems presented in this chapter. If, on the other hand, it is found that whilst past and present government policies have contributed to teacher deprofessionalisation, there is still a lack of interest in these areas, then the evidence would begin to suggest that some of the blame for the state of affairs described above needs to be located within the teaching profession itself. It is to this question that the next chapter turns.

4

IMPOVERISHING A SENSE OF PROFESSIONALISM

Who's to blame?

Introduction

The education and training of teachers are crucial to the quality of any society. Teachers are the gate-keepers of its traditions and culture and facilitators of its evolution. They contribute to the emotional, social and moral development of the young as well as stimulating their minds and furnishing them with skills, for their own, their society's and humanity's benefit. ... For teachers, above all professionals, must, almost by definition, be intellectually active, authoritative, lively, critical, reflective, flexible and ever attentive to the constant and changing demands of the young and the society for which they are being prepared.

(General Teaching Council Trust (1993), section F, paras 1 and 4)

There is much to admire in the above quotation, pointing as it does to the role of teaching professionals as guardians of culture, as well as guides in young people's search for maturity in both personal and social terms. It is difficult to overestimate such a role. It is not surprising then that the qualities such professionals will need, which the quotation goes on to describe, are of a kind readily approved by any proponent of a society based on rationality, democracy, and justice. Teachers' professional development and education, then, are crucial to the quality of any society. However, the previous chapter arrived at the conclusion that there is a substantial limiting of teachers' vision at the present time. The cause of this was interpreted as being largely governmental, but with the real possibility of teacher compliance. Nevertheless, one must be careful that a too-simplistic picture is not drawn. To depict this problem as simply one of government direction or teachers' complicity would be to do precisely that. It is important initially to re-visit some of the themes raised in earlier chapters and point out that the whole of this debate is contextualised by wider themes. When this is established, it will be possible to ask questions about teacher complicity.

Over the last ten to fifteen years, five major forces, an historical consciousness, a critical professional literature, free-market thought, post-modern influences and post-Fordist movements, have impinged upon teachers and teacher education, and upon accepted understandings of professionalism. It is possible to argue that these forces have made the realisation of any professional ideal problematical.

Historical consciousness

A first force is the criticism that in many welfare states professionals have, since the Second World War, monopolised services for their own benefit rather than providing the kind of service to clients that one might expect. In medicine, Williamson (1992), for instance, describes an evolving awareness by 'clients' of medical practice in the United Kingdom. These clients, like their counterparts in the United States, are now much less likely than before to accept medical perceptions and standards as those that should alone define a situation, and are increasingly vocal in the belief that these need to be contested and re-defined in the light of their and other client perceptions. Similarly, research suggests (MORI 1994) that whilst, in 1989, 75% of the UK general public thought that the police could be trusted, this had dropped to 66% by 1994. Finally, accusations over the alleged teaching of dangerously progressive ideas in the 1960s (Cox and Dyson 1970) were closely followed by suggestions that teachers could not be trusted to run schools properly (Auld 1980). This increased questioning of the teaching profession's actions and intentions in England was solidified in many people's minds in the mid-1980s by hostile newspaper coverage of the bitter strikes. Such heightened consciousness has provided the background within which professionals generally have increasingly come to be seen as self- rather than as other-serving.

A critical professional literature

This more sceptical perception by the public appears to have had two consequences at the theoretical level, both of which have been touched on in earlier chapters. One is the movement in the literature upon professionalism. Freidson (1984) suggests that a watershed in the academic literature can be seen in the 1960s. Formerly, the literature concentrated on the definition of professionals, by fairly uncritically accepting the professionals' adherence to a code of ethics designed to place the client at the centre of concern, through descriptions of the life and work of individual paragons (e.g. Carr-Saunders and Wilson 1933). Since then, there has developed an increasingly critical stance, which sees professionalism as but a manifestation of occupational strategy aimed at monopolising practices, leading to increased power and financial reward (Collins 1990). Whilst this is clearly not the whole story –

Abbott (1983), for instance, argues that professional ethics are based upon a mixture of both altruism and self-interest – yet there seems little doubt that this increasingly sharp edge in the descriptions of professionals affects a more general consciousness.

The development of free-market thought

A second consequence at the theoretical level in this critical professional literature, was an explosion of free-market literature. This, as we have seen, suggested that only by means of competition between different providers could the quality of service to clients be assured; and only by such changes could clients come to see themselves as discerning and critical purchasers of goods, and not recipients of services, at the mercy of professional whim (Friedman 1962, Graham and Clarke 1986, Chubb and Moe 1990, Osborne and Gaebler 1992). It was on the back of such thought that public-service teachers were faced with a legislative agenda which included measures such as facilitating parents moving their children to different schools, to schools changing their governing status, greater financial devolution, and formula funding. All of these have been intended to increase client access to a greater quantity and variety of schools. They have also increasingly placed the responsibility for the recruitment of students squarely onto teachers' shoulders. Moreover, by casting professionals in a commercial light – individuals or occupations selling their 'services' – it again effectively reduces their status within society from being disinterested and/or altruistic, to yet another salesperson out to sell their wares – and therefore the suggestion was that *caveat emptor* should apply here just as much as it would in any other market-place. Furthermore, it should be clear by now that whilst, under the New Modernisers, the function of the market has been relegated much more to a subsidiary place in the overall scheme of things, most of the legislative measures enacted in the heyday of free-market ideology are still in place, and it continues to have the kinds of influence seen then – only now other, more recent influences need to be added.

Post-modern influences

If two sources of theoretical pressure upon professionals have been the free-market and professional literatures, a third, more subtle, but still powerful influence has been the move from a 'modernist' to a 'post-modernist' view of knowledge and the social world. An increasing scepticism of the 'enlightenment project' – the ability of humankind through a universal reason to transcend the particularities of time and culture and fashion a concept of progress suitable for all humanity – has led to the view that such 'grand narratives' are no longer plausible (Lyotard 1984). The best one can do in such circumstances is to accept the inevitability of the 'situatedness' of one's existence, and of the framing of one's experience. This then calls into question the possibility or wisdom of social engineering, of overarching norms and values (Green 1994). The most plausible approach can only be one of localised arrangements between parties knowing and living within particular circumstances. A commitment to an overarching set of professional norms – save those that might appeal to or give a guarantee to a potential client – is increasingly called into question (Carr 1995). It is easy to see how such pessimistic relativism can feed into either a diseased Conservatism ('why try to change anything – we can never know what anything "better" would look like, because these can be no more than discredited grand narratives') or into a virulent free-market stance ('there can be no meta-ethic to judge upon encounters – so leave such mechanisms to market forces'). On either count, the prognosis for professionals is deeply pessimistic, for neither can accept the possibility of validating the existence of a set of ethics, nor of providing a vision of a good society within which a professional body ultimately needs to locate its practice.

Post-Fordist movements

A final force, underpinning much of the New Modernisers' agenda, is the general movement within Western societies from a 'Fordist' to a 'post-Fordist' production base. This movement stems both from the relative failure of Fordist production systems themselves, as well as from the greater opportunities for differentiation of production and surveillance, offered by increased micro-technological progress (Amin 1994). Whilst it seems clear that this is a process that is not complete – there are still many sites of production that have most of the characteristics of Fordism – yet it has been argued that this movement is rapidly being adopted by the economies of the more technologically advanced nations. It impacts on professionals because one of its key concepts is the notion of the devolution of responsibility but not power. Policy will then be determined at the centre, whilst its implementation (including responsibility for the efficient utilisation of allocated finance) will be devolved to the periphery – the 'units' of schools, hospitals, GP fundholder, police stations, etc., in the public sector (Smyth 1993). Within such a scenario, as described above, a 'New Public Management' (Hood 1991) will be a necessary tool, and will effectively exclude professionals – and professional bodies – from policy determination. Their position will be located at the interface with management; expert advice on how and where finance should be allocated, on the most client-friendly responses, on the major priorities for implementation. Professionals, however, will not be co-partners in policy, nor even participants, and increasingly their professional bodies will not be welcomed for their opinions on, for example, the role of health, education, policing, etc., where management or politicians feel they can exclude them.

Key criteria for professionals such as autonomy and expertise will also be increasingly circumscribed to fit in with centralist agendas.

These forces, ranging from the purely theoretical to the intensely practical, result, whether intentionally or not, in demands for both a centralisation, as well as a decentralisation of power. Just as paradoxically, they also lead to an increased emphasis upon a bureaucratisation of functioning as well as the de-bureaucratisation of other functions. The first has led to legislation curtailing teacher discretion in terms of curriculum and testing, as well as tightening central surveillance through target setting, testing and Ofsted inspections. The second results in free-market legislation, such as open enrolment, and opting out, and local financial management, intended to lead to greater consumer choice, more local responsiveness, and the curtailment of absolute professional power.

Now this is not to argue that some measure of centralisation or decentralisation is inappropriate in the case of professional functioning. Indeed, it seems dangerously optimistic to assume that professionals, given a free hand, would constantly deliver a quality service to clients, and would automatically cast the development of their practice within a vision that is in the best interests of society as a whole. Previous experience does not appear to support such optimism.

Nevertheless, it should be clear by now that there are considerable dangers in either curtailing the functioning of professionals such that their survival depends upon satisfying the whims of particular groups of 'customers', or by legislation such that they simply become functionaries, Taylorian 'technical rationalists'. In the former case, they may become individuals devoid of the right or the ability to form judgements consonant with wider 'public' or 'ecological' roles, in the latter to develop practice upon the basis of new situations, that they have to rely upon a script devised by some other authority in order to function. Schön (1983) in his discussion of reflective practice, and other writers on this topic (Van Manen 1977, Zeichner and Liston 1987, Eraut 1995) have all stressed the necessary requirement for true professionals to have precisely this ability if they are to deal with new situations in an intelligent and adaptable manner, simply because their practice cannot be scripted in advance, reliant upon some technical bible of suitable remedies to clients' problems. Instead, professionals need to ground their practice in terms of an ability to recast their theories, using the insights of others, including their clients, in an intelligent, self-critical, and ultimately unpredictable manner. Yet, the drive towards competence training in the United States, United Kingdom and Australasia (see McNamara 1992, Prain 1995, and Halliday 1995), specifying as it does in advance what makes for a 'competent' professional, suggests that this is the road that these societies are taking. Later, in Chapter 6, the limitations of competency-based approaches for professional preparation will be examined in closer detail.

Which of the various roles available, then, is the teaching profession preparing itself and being prepared for: a democratic, critical, and emancipating role or a functional, 'market-driven' or 'technical rational' role? In the previous chapter, evidence was presented which suggested that within such provision there was a lack of focus or attention on either the 'public' or the 'ecological' dimensions of teachers' practice. Furthermore the research suggested that professional development education was characterised by:

- implementation, skill-based matters at a level of 'technical rationality'
- short-termism
- 'just-in-time' training
- training, not education
- absence of macro-social considerations
- lack of critical input
- heavy central direction.

Such matters led to the conclusion that under the influence of government policy stressing issues of implementation, teachers were neglecting these vital dimensions of the public and ecological natures of the role. It was further suggested that if teachers and schools continued to lower their heads to pull their classroom or management carts, it should come as no surprise if they ended up at destinations they did not select; a simple description of deprofessionalisation.

However, whilst the evidence appeared to point to an externally imposed deprofessionalisation – UK governments of the last fifteen years have pursued educational policies based extensively upon a mixture of free-market and post-Fordist strategies – yet this did not prove that such teacher attitudes were the simple result of such policies. It might be that such attitudes would exist even were governments to pursue other, more professional-friendly policies.

This chapter explores this more worrying possibility. To that end, a further exploration of the data already collected from the LEA-maintained, the GM and independent sectors was mounted. The idea was to determine whether the greater degrees of management and curricular freedom enjoyed by the latter two sectors was reflected in a greater interest in the provision of professional development education in the 'public' and 'ecological' dimensions than that displayed in the LEA schools. If, as was implied earlier, it was pressure from government policies that was leading to such a strong focus on implementation, then the data should reveal a greater emphasis upon wider professional dimensions in professional development education choices in the GM and independent sectors than in the LEA sector, since the first two enjoy comparatively greater freedom from government policy and intervention.

The rationale for this investigation was initially quite similar to that described in Chapter 2. Data reported from the school management plans for the first two years of the study permitted an assessment of the range of topic areas and what level of diversity existed between sectors. A similar assessment of in-service topics posited for the ensuing two years enabled the making of comparisons over the four years to see whether or not the earlier diversity had been maintained and whether or not any trends were emerging.

Data collected from the second part of the questionnaire permitted an examination of the perceptions of the location of sources of pressure for choices in professional development education. In the light of the hypothesis that the GM and independent sectors enjoyed greater curricular and managerial freedoms from government interventions, central to this analysis would be the need to see whether or not, over the four-year period, any diversity and difference between sectors was significant. To pursue this enquiry still further, the data on the perceived strength of pressure from nine areas of influence were explored to see if there was evidence to support the view that there would be greater diversity between the three sectors.

In a third and final analysis, data on the average length of courses attended and reasons for the choice of this length of course were examined again to see whether or not the greater curricular and managerial freedoms of the GM and independent sectors resulted in greater diversity. These data should also allow some conclusions to be drawn about whether or not these two sectors were seeking longer courses of a sort that would permit reflection on the 'public' and 'ecological' dimensions of teacher preparation which this book advocates.

With regard to the first area, which was concerned with the priorities for professional development education in the first two years, the priorities discussed in this chapter refer to the priorities of a school sector as a whole, rather than any one school's individual priorities. Nevertheless, it does not seem unreasonable to assume some degree of linkage between overall popularity of an area of professional development education within a school sector, and its importance to individual schools within this sector.

As already reported in Chapter 2, across the three sectors, a total of 51 priority areas were identified for the first two years under study and 53 areas for the second two years. Table 4.1 reports the sector topic total responses.

The frequency with which each area was indicated by schools was totalled and a prioritised list for professional development education topics by both

Table 4.1 Number of in-service topics identified by sectors

Sector	n	Number of discrete choices given	
		1992–4	1995–7
LEA	28	27	26
GM	28	34	32
Independent	29	26	33
Total	85	51	53

Table 4.2 Ranked in-service sector priorities (1992–4)

Ranking	LEA maintained	GM	Independent	Overall
1	NC/subject 69%	NC/subject 71%	NC/subject 74%	NC/subject 71%
2	Management 59%	IT 46%	Pastoral care 33%	Management 38%
3	IT 45%	Management 39%	Appraisal 22%	IT 37%
4	Assessment 41%	Differentiation 36%	Ofsted 18%	Differentiation 26%
5	Differentiation 34%	SEN 32%	IT 18%	Pastoral care 24%

sector and for the overall sample was compiled. The top five areas are shown in Table 4.2. Percentages in this table, then, describe the number of times an area was chosen by all of the schools in that sector.

In terms of the data, a number of things need to be noticed. The first is that in the first five rankings across the three sectors, there were nine different topics. Of these, two topics, those concerned with National Curriculum/ subject and Information Technology were common to all three sectors. Two further topics, Management and Differentiation, were common to two sectors. Finally, there were four topics that appear in the LEA and GM sectors but not in the independent sector. Three topics, Pastoral Care, Appraisal and Ofsted, were peculiar to the independent sector at this level of priority.

At first sight, these data might be interpreted in line with the original hypothesis, that the three sectors show increasing diversity as one moves from the LEA to the independent sectors. Certainly the independent sector's priorities look distinct from the other two. By contrast, four out of five of the top priorities of the LEA and GM sectors are shared, whereas the independent sector shares only two out of its five with either of the other two sectors.

If such dissimilarity or diversity suggests difference, then a closer look at the topics themselves suggests a rather different interpretation. The topics that are different in the independent sector's top five are Pastoral Care, Appraisal and Ofsted. If the diversity suggests a possibility for consideration of professional issues and considerations, then the actual choice of topics runs counter to such an argument. Thus, developmental work on appraisal is invariably described as training rather than as education for appraisers and appraisees. Similarly, preparation for Ofsted is very often of the 'just-in-time' training style (particularly as schools are usually given no more than six months' notice of such an inspection). Pastoral Care might allow some scope for consideration of wider professional issues through some of the topics in the personal and social education curriculum, but there is little evidence to suggest that this occurs. Furthermore, it should be noted that well over four-fifths of independent-sector courses were still of the one-day variety (see below), and therefore were unlikely to allow development of the kind of issues and principles that this book suggests are important for professional development. Finally, the high priority given to subject/National Curriculum and Management as professional development education topics may not surprise many but they will consume much professional development time and money and will limit opportunities for developing an appreciation of the public and ecological aspects of teaching.

The picture, then, that emerges from the data for the first two-year period of professional development education does not give much cause for optimism that in any sector wider professional issues were being given much time, space or priority. In terms of sector priorities for professional development education for the second two-year period, respondents were similarly asked to indicate which areas they anticipated would inform their professional development work. As noted above (see Table 4.1), the total of 53 priority areas was very similar to that for the first two years (51). There were, however, 24 new areas, with a similar number of areas dropping out. Over the four-year period, then, a total of 75 professional development choices were identified. The ranked priorities for the second two-year period between the three sectors are shown in Table 4.3.

The data in Table 4.3 indicate that there had been a reduction in the diversity of choice in the first five priorities across all three sectors. Only eight different topics are reported in the first five priority rankings and now three topics are common to all three sectors. As before, there were four out of five priorities shared between the two maintained sectors and now there were three shared by them with the independent sector. The trend then actually appears to be one of less diversity. The two topics in the independent sector's list that were not common to the other two sectors were again Pastoral Care and Ofsted, and the same comments about the limited nature of their involvement in the public and ecological areas can be made here again. Furthermore, the

Table 4.3 Ranked professional development education sector priorities (1995–7)

Rank	LEA maintained	GM	Independent	Overall
1	NC/subject (52%)	NC/subject (55%)	NC/subject (52%)	NC/subject (53%)
2	Management (45%)	IT (48%)	Pastoral care (28%)	IT (30%)
3	Assessment (31%)	Differentiation (26%)	Ofsted (24%)	Management (30%)
4	SEN (27%)	SEN (26%)	Management training (29%)	SEN (20%)
5	IT (24%)	Management (22%)	IT (16%)	Assessment (18%)

three priorities shared by all three sectors, these being subject/National Curriculum, Information Technology and Management, do not, in a context of short, one-day courses, represent places where the opportunity for critical analysis, reflection and wider professional issues could be developed.

There was, then, diminishing diversity between the sectors in their top professional development priority areas and those topics unique to the independent sector's rankings were not topics that easily lend themselves to arguments in support of wider, ecological professional concerns. Any hope that the independent sector would reveal a significantly different set of priorities, indicating a weakening of government directives and evidence of the greater provision of the 'ecological' and 'public' dimensions of teacher development, appear to be refuted by these data.

The three sectors' perceptions of sources of pressure for professional development education

As well as asking what priorities the schools had, and whether these were changing, it was also considered important to ask the respondents whether they felt their priorities for professional development education were driven by external pressures, internal pressures, or a combination of both. Such consideration by schools of their perceived sources of pressures would, it was believed, provide a useful indicator of their interest in wider, macro-social issues in professional development. Their responses over the four-year period showing the division between external, internal or a combination of both sources of pressure are given in Table 4.4.

Within the three sectors, these data revealed somewhat contrasting differences of view. No particular view appeared to be consistent across all three sectors. In both the GM and independent sectors, and with little

Table 4.4 Perceptions of sources of pressure for in-service (1992–4 and 1995–7)

Source	LEA		GM		Ind.		Total		%	
	L2	N2	L2	N2	L2	N2	L2	N2	L2	N2
External	4	4	4	1	3	2	11	7	13%	8%
Internal	7	17	1	1	9	5	17	23	19%	26%
Both	16	7	22	26	18	21	56	54	64%	62%
No reply	1	0	1	0	1	3	3	3	3%	3%
Total (*n*)	28	28	28	28	31	31	87	87	99%	99%

Note:
L2 (last two years) = 1992–4, N2 (next two years) = 1995–7

difference in emphasis, there appeared to be a sense that in the future, pressures would be a combination of both the internal and the external. More striking was the change in the LEA sector. Here the perception was of internal pressure being more important and much less of a combination of both. What appeared to be consistently low across all three sectors, however, was the strength of external influences. In the light of a main hypothesis of this book, that as a profession, teachers are failing to consider the wider macro-social, 'ecological' and cultural ramifications of practice, the perception of the weakness of external factors is worrying. In order to test this further and to elicit extra information, more detailed analyses were made of data relating to nine specific factors that might impinge on professional development education. The nine factors were:

- external legislative requirements
- business pressures
- parental pressures
- community concerns
- competition from other schools
- staff personal demand
- school curriculum innovation
- pupil needs
- subject updating.

As in Chapter 2, schools were asked to rank each factor according to a six-point scale indicating strength of influence, with 1 representing very strong influence and 6 very weak influence.

In the light of the main hypothesis of this chapter, that there should be greater differences between the sectors, which reflect greater autonomy and therefore scope to examine these wider professional issues and considerations, a one-way analysis of variance and a Kruskal–Wallis test were performed yielding identical results. This was conducted in order to determine whether and in what respect there were any significant differences between the sectors. At the 10% level, significant differences were found only in respect of legislative influence, competition and curriculum for the first two-year period and for the second two-year period significant differences between the sectors were found only for competition and curriculum. No significant differences, then, existed for seven of the nine factors in any of the three sectors for the second two-year period. This represents a trend towards less diversity between the sectors. The analysis of legislative, competitive and curricular influence in the earlier years indicated that whilst the independent sector's view of legislative influence had been significantly different from the other two sectors at the 10% level, this position was not upheld for the next two years, and supported notions of convergence between the sectors.

This finding is particularly interesting, for if all three sectors were paying increasing attention to legislation in the later two years, this would be correlative, perhaps even causal evidence, that legislation was depressing interest in the 'public' and 'ecological' dimensions. However, as the independent sector had not, until this time, seen legislation as a significant pressure, and as their interest in the 'public' and 'ecological' dimensions had been no stronger for the first two-year period than it was for the second, this tends to undermine the view that government legislation on the maintained sector was wholly responsible for fostering deprofessionalising attitudes and approaches in provision for professional development education.

Further, with respect to the analysis of the data for competition during the first two-year period, and the second two-year period, it was clear that whilst schools in the GM sector had joined those in the independent sector in seeing competition as a significant pressure, there was no developing divergence between the three sectors as a whole. Indeed, indications from other findings suggested that convergence continued to be more the norm.

What of the last area of significant difference, that of curriculum? Data here seem to reinforce the picture that emerged from earlier data that the level of diversity in professional development priorities between sectors had not increased. Indeed the means for each sector (see Table 2.5) indicated an increase in the perception of the strength of curricular influence in INSET activities – a more strongly school-focused task.

What then appeared important from these analyses was that the more ostensibly external pressures (reflecting the macro-social issues) on professional development education choices were not significantly different between the sectors. Neither does the picture give any clear evidence of a trend of greater divergence appearing between the sectors. These two points then combine to undermine the hypothesis that the greater curricular and managerial freedoms of the GM and independent sectors generated more interest in the 'ecological' and 'public' dimensions of teaching.

Length of INSET courses across the sectors

As a final area of investigation, respondents were asked to indicate the length of courses that their staff attended and which were funded from the school's own resources for professional development education. If factors such as critical reflection, analysis, making judgements, and wider contextual thought were seen as necessary for true professional practice, then one might argue that there should have been a range of course lengths. If the principal rationale was instead more 'just-in-time' training and issues of implementation, and serious critical consideration of the issues involved was not part of the agenda, then it seems reasonable to believe that less time would be spent upon the actual amount of professional development education required, and the time it took. The data (Tables 2.1 and 2.2) for each sector on this issue revealed the heavy domination by schools of the use of the one-day course, as indicated by 91% of respondents. This does not augur well for a situation or for a professional need for teachers to reflect critically and think more widely. The data do reveal, however, that as one moves through the sectors, there was a small decline in this domination and a corresponding increase towards the independent sector in courses that were slightly longer. When the data for the reasons for choosing particular course lengths were examined, however, they still tended to reinforce a picture dominated by practicalities, budgets and an absence of content issues. Thus it was clear from the data that three major criteria were used in the choice of courses: what providers offered; the cost/time involved; and the disruption caused by such courses. It was also clear that each sector reacted differently. Thus, cost and time constraints (37%) were the strongest influences in the LEA-maintained sector. This was not too surprising, given that budgetary constraints were strong, and cost (and shortage of cash) centrally imposed. Nevertheless, it should be noted that both other factors played equally quite prominent roles (28%) in this sector. The situation in the GM sector was quite different. Here, cost and time were very minor constraints (9%) as were considerations of disruption (26%). In this case, issues of what providers offered were much more prominent (53%). Again, the situation differed for that of the independent sector. Whilst considerations of cost and time were slight (16%), and issues of what providers offered were also not large (24%), twice as much consideration (49%) was given to questions of disruption.

Given the domination of the one-day course, even in the independent sector (84%), the reasons for choosing it as shown between sectors do not suggest that greater professional autonomy and independence can be seen by moving across the sectors from LEA through GM to independent. Certainly, each sector appeared to have its own distinct rationale for choosing this short form of course. In the LEA sector, cost was paramount (37%) though not by a long way; in the GM what providers offered was top (53%); and disruption (49%)was highest in the thinking of the independent sector. However, none of the three reasons offered by each sector seems remotely conducive to the sort of 'professional development' argued for in this book.

If, in the LEA sector, cost was the prime consideration, this would seem to be indicative of a considerable lack of autonomy as budget constraints are nationally set. If going for one-day course options was the main form of provision then this does not augur well for wider, critical, reflective professional development embracing macro-social issues.

It should also be noted that, as in Chapter 2, there seems to be circularity in the reasons given by schools in the GM sector concerning 'what providers offer'. Thus, were the courses taken because they were the kind of courses GM schools really wanted, and because providers were market sensitive enough to know this? Or would the GM sector really have preferred longer provision but found themselves stymied by providers who were insensitive to their needs? Either way, professional issues cannot be fully explored and developed.

In the independent sector, whilst it is true that up to 16% of courses were over one day in length, nevertheless the prime reason for choice of course length given in this sector was to avoid 'disruption'. This was so much the case that two schools indicated that only professional development education that was offered in school vacations would be considered, as otherwise their teachers were removed from classes that parents were paying for. Again no ostensibly 'professional development' reason emerged in this sector, and, where there was greater opportunity for choice, the one-day course still received 84% support.

It would appear, in summary, that the main context for professional development education activities across all sectors was the one-day course; that reasons for this varied between sectors but all contained significant degrees of pragmatism rather than professional development. To find professional development education so dominated by this kind of course is worrying and it must be asked whether this can be a healthy situation in the dominant profession of an education service in a democracy.

Conclusions

A key rationale in this chapter has been to see if teachers' deprofessionalisation perceived in the state sector, and especially LEA schools, through short-term, 'implementationist' professional development education could be attributed to government policy. If it was, it was argued that analysis of the same factors in the GM and independent sectors would yield differing conclusions, as these schools were, and still are, less subject to the impositions of government policy than the LEA sector. The data analysed in this survey only partially support this view. Whilst there were differences in terms of emphasis on curricular and competitive aspects of schools policy, there were many similarities between the sectors in terms of the length of courses, and the topics in priority lists.

A first conclusion, then, must be that whilst government policies may be contributing to teacher deprofessionalisation, this cannot be the full story. Instead, there would seem to be an absence on the part of schools and teachers within them to seek a deeper understanding of what being a professional teacher entails. This failure by schools to recognise and provide appropriate professional development education to enhance such discussion and appreciation, cannot help to develop and enhance the profession.

A second conclusion is that deprofessionalisation cannot be a concern of the state sector alone. If, as this book argues, and as the majority of schools in the private sector, and teachers within them claim, they are committed to an ideal of public service, they also need a similar appreciation of the 'public' and 'ecological' dimensions of professional practice as those in the state sector. Yet they appear to neglect these issues in their professional development activities quite as much as their colleagues do in the state sector. It is hard to see how teachers in any sector can claim a strong commitment to these ideals if they spend so little of their professional development time thinking about them, or about the macro-social issues that impinge upon them.

Thirdly, an acceptance of such dimensions within the professional development of teachers has implications beyond their mere contemplation. Giving serious consideration to the 'ecological' dimension of teaching would involve teachers in understanding and discussing social, economic and political trends, and their impact upon education. This greatly extends the scope, time and expense of professional development education provision and professional development, and would therefore require extra funding or, more likely, the re-allocation of funding. Similarly, giving serious consideration to the 'public' dimension of teaching would seem, necessarily, to involve consideration of questions of equity in schooling, and where, as with the case of private education, quality of provision is largely determined on the basis of parental income, this would seem to have the potential to raise profound ethical questions not only about the role of teachers, but about the role that education plays – or could play – in the distribution of life chances within a society. Teachers in the state sector may feel these are issues beyond their immediate concern, some in the private sector may feel they are issues they would rather not face – but it seems implicit within any notion of the kind of 'extended' professionalism we propose that their discussion and appreciation are essential. Teachers may choose to pull their curriculum carts without raising their heads to look at the road they are travelling – but then they will almost certainly end up as mere 'technical rationalists' or deliverers of transient consumer taste, or a combination of both. However, if they choose to engage in debate about the roads their profession should head down, it will not necessarily be a comfortable one.

Finally, and importantly, whilst this chapter suggests that not only is government legislation hastening teacher deprofessionalisation, it has not established the precise reasons for teachers' compliance in this project. This will be discussed at some length later in the book, but for the moment, and for what it is worth, there is little evidence to suggest that this is done intentionally. Rather, it may well be due as much to the hierarchical and bureaucratic nature and functioning of most schools. There is plenty of evidence to support the contention that bureaucracy has precisely the effect of allocating positions within an organisation – and particularly in schools – that are minutely described and circumscribed, and which entice individuals into taking limited and restricted views of the organisation's functioning, both internally, and in its interface with other organisations and the society at large (Anderson 1968, Armytage 1970, Pusey 1976, Katz 1977, Kelman and Hamilton 1989, Bottery 1992). If this is the case, then the challenge of beginning to remedy the problem may be as much by changing the structures and functioning of educational institutions as with either consciousness raising in the teaching profession, or pressing for more professional-friendly legislation.

However, the immediate concern is with the activities of teachers in schools, and how they prioritise them. In this context, a crucial area and period for teachers' professional time is in their first few months, as they are trained and inducted into the teaching profession. What experiences are they given, what guidance is suggested, what topics are dealt with in their initial few months? A crucial figure – some would say the crucial figure – is the mentor, the individual with the institutional responsibility for overseeing their training and induction within the school. The next chapter examines the critical role of the mentor in the development of new teachers in order to see what kinds of messages are being passed on here.

5

PERCEPTIONS OF PROFESSIONALISM BY THE MENTORS OF STUDENT TEACHERS

Introduction

This book has made clear its sympathy for the situation of many teachers today. From being perceived – and perceiving themselves – as central players in the grand social engineering project called the welfare state, consulted on its expansion and shape, facilitated by conciliatory management and politics in operating it, they have come to find themselves increasingly marginalised from the policy process, increasingly distrusted by media and the general public, and being invited to provide no more than their technical expertise within managerial strategies and policies devised elsewhere. As Pollitt (1992) so trenchantly remarked, professionals are nowadays much more likely to be 'on tap' than 'on top'.

Public professionals of all kinds will recognise the symptoms of this spectrum of distrust, and teachers as forcefully as any. The stress, the overwork, the early retirements, the nervous breakdowns, the financial cutbacks, the lack of recognition of their worth, the lowered morale, the reduction in their role, the legislative and managerial impositions – these are all symptomatic of the views of professionals described above. What is perhaps even more worrying for some professionals is that if they thought that changes of government might alter the way in which they are treated, they may well need to limit their optimism, for whilst it would be wrong to say that there is now a coalescence of view about the professional across the political spectrum, yet the trend of thinking from a diversity of political viewpoints results in similarly sceptical views about them.

It has already been noted that this change in attitude towards professionals is normally associated with the works of radical right-wing thinkers from think tanks like the Institute of Economic Affairs, from writers like Friedman (1962), Hayek (1973), and from the public-choice school of Niskanen (1971) and Downs (1967). Indeed, Deakin (1987, p. 177) sees the general acceptance of their case as 'among the New Right's most striking intellectual achievements'. Their arguments, or variations on them, are now well known. The strategy of delivering welfare through the employment of autonomous professionals in welfare-state bureaucracies is inefficient and ineffective, because it becomes producer led, it generates a nationally debilitating dependency culture, it produces big-brother bureaucracies, and it inevitably leads to politicians taking short-term vote-catching decisions rather than those in the general public's best interests.

However, it would be wrong to see such hostility to traditional professional practice as coming only from the right. Table 5.1 suggests that professionals nowadays face a much fuller spectrum of political hostility. Marxists, for example, have long argued that welfare states are the results of class conflict, being little more than strategies by which capital has 'bought off' workers, and professionals have been part of this cosy arrangement. As long ago as 1934, Laski wrote (p. 149) that:

> social legislation is not the outcome of a rational and objective willing of the common good by all members of the community alike; it is the price paid for those legal principles which secure the predominance of the owners of their prosperity. It is the body of concessions offered to avert a decisive challenge to the challenge by which their authority is maintained.

Other, more modern writers are largely in agreement. Ginsburg (1979, p. 2) argues that the welfare state 'remains part of a capitalist state which is fundamentally concerned with the maintenance and reproduction of capitalist social relations'. Now, in the late twentieth century, with the inter-nationalisation of capital, and the ability to play off one national workforce against another, it is argued that the capitalist class no longer needs to buy off the workers. Professionals then are either willing colluders in the oppression of the working public, or gullible fools who will be (and are being) dispensed with now that their usefulness has passed. Their future is that of other workers, their only role, if they wish to remain central players, that of the overthrow of the capitalist order.

Socialists, and especially Fabian socialists, have seen the welfare state in a much more positive light, as an ideal vehicle for the gradual, non-violent transformation of society towards one of much greater equality. For Tawney (1931, p. 182), for instance, equality was the 'necessary corollary ... of the Christian conception of man'. But even within such a vision, professionals do not come out well, for like right-wing thinkers, socialists today may also see professionals as likely to usurp welfare services for their own ends, which can lead only to a disempowered citizenry, and to an ineffective and inefficient way of delivering welfare, health and education. The way forward for them is for a vigorous managerialism – for professionals to be audited, assessed, and accountable to external bodies, and proactive managers; the disempowerment must be of professionals, not of the citizenry.

Table 5.1 Ideological challenges to professional practice

Viewpoint	Key phrase	Reasons for change	Winners	Losers	Ultimate professional role	Professional response
Marxist	'those in power no longer need to …'	If in the past capital needed to buy off workers by means of welfare states, with the internationalisation of money and markets, the ability to play off one national workforce against another, it no longer needs to do this.	Capital	Recipients Producers Workers	Memebers of impoverished safety net welfare provision: or like other workers subject to vagaries and whims of international capital.	Protest, conflict, potential action ultimate objective of overthrow of capitalist system.
Pluralist	'no longer can afford to'	Because of increased competition from abroad, rising costs and negative demographic changes, countries can no longer afford to run fully fledged welfare states.		Recipients Producers	Impoverished second-class professionals in comparison with private colleagues, always tempted to make the move to private practice.	Political involvement, fighting for welfare state; institutional financial involvement; education of clients as to current provision.
Radical Liberal	'… not the most effective means of delivering welfare'	The strategy of providing delivery of welfare through autonomous professionals is ineffective, becomes producer-led, makes big-brother bureaucracies, generates a nationally debilitating dependency culture.	Recipients	Producers	A seller and marketer of quality products to discerning customers.	Promoter of public good over private interest; incorporator of client into professional process along with their education.

			Recipients	Producers	
Socialist	'... not the most effective means of delivering welfare ...'	Autonomous professionals will tend to usurp services for their own ends; it leads to disempowered citizenry, and consequently is not the most effective means of delivering welfare.		To be audited, assessed and accountable to external bodies and professional managers.	Proactive response of overt professional responsibility involving change of role and incorporation of client views and their education.
Pragmatic political	'... not the most politically sophisticated means of delivering welfare ...'	Politicians realise the advantages of post-Fordist production techniques transferred to the welfare state, and devolve responsibility for implementation while retaining power, in so doing cutting out the middle tiers and deflecting blame to implementers.	Politicians Recipients Producers?	Producers? To be technical implementers of policy carefully managed most probably in a market scenario.	Structered professional development on welfare state issues; education of clients; political involvement of policy level.

However, criticisms of professional practice do not end there. Moving towards the centre of the political spectrum, the pluralist will not see the welfare state as a purely residual mechanism, as the radical right does, nor will it be seen as a bribe as the Marxist does, nor again will it be seen as necessarily needing to be universal in its provision as the socialist does. Rather, the pluralist will argue that because of increased competition from abroad, rising costs and negative demographic changes (an ageing population, and a smaller tax base to support welfare services), the country simply cannot afford a fully fledged welfare state. What will be provided will only be that which is affordable; any expansion in its provision will be dependent upon economic growth. Furthermore, whilst it may be the duty of the state to finance what is affordable, it is not necessarily its duty to provide it. As Meacher said (1992, p. 91): 'A new model of service delivery is therefore needed. It should discriminate neither for nor against either the public or the private sectors, but use whichever maximises accountability for the individual, without regard to income, and for all equally.'

On this scenario, professionals employed within the public sector, may, unless economic conditions dramatically improve, always be penny-pinching, and trying to make do with resources that never seem to stretch far enough; second-class professionals compared to their colleagues in the private sector, ultimately tempted to join them, in conditions that are more pleasant, better funded and better paid – though here too, there will be an increased concern with costs and accountability.

Indeed, if one combines the perspective of the political pluralist with the actions of the political pragmatist, professionals may feel even more dissatisfied with their lot. The pragmatist will realise the political advantages in a post-Fordist strategy of devolving responsibility to individuals at the institutional level, whilst retaining control of finance and policy at the centre. In this way they can increasingly pass work and worry down to those at the periphery – the teacher, the doctor, the nurse, the social worker, the police – whilst also attributing blame for policy failings and financial inadequacies to them as well. Life for the professional then becomes harder and more unpleasant, as both work and lack of control of their work increase. Further, and as we have seen, if the political pragmatist borrows the rhetoric of the far right, and introduces competition at the institutional level, either within a purely internal market, or one that demands competition between both the public and the private sectors, a further degree of insecurity is added to the life of the professional. The welfare state is not regarded then as residual, as a bribe, affordable, or universal, but simply as politically manageable – taking the form that most suits the political purpose of keeping the lid on problems, of deflecting blame, of staying in power.

All professionals, but teachers in particular, need to realise that the world has changed, and they need to be much more aware of these changes, to be much more proactive in the debate about where their future role lies. A vital question, then, is: are they? Are teachers aware of the underlying causes of their present discomforts, and are they taking steps through the provision of appropriate initial training, and continuing professional development, to debate seriously the future of their profession? Are they not only providing a quality service to their clients, but also changing both themselves and government/managerial policies to do this? If the answer to these questions is in the negative, then one would be bound to say that they are being de-professionalised.

The earlier chapters in this book, which examined aspects of continuing professional development among serving teachers, found that there were worrying signs of this deprofessionalisation. This was evidenced in particular through the kind of professional development education courses attended by teachers, by the limited length of these courses, and by the particular stress on implementation and work which quite closely resembled 'just-in-time training' so favoured in industrial training quality manuals. This might be a suitable approach for ensuring that stocks of a product are kept at the minimum level to ensure maximum profitability, but one that is singularly unsuited for the development of sophisticated professional practice. What was noticeable by its absence from such professional development education was any stress on wider issues of professionalism, with a focus on what we have termed the 'public' and 'ecological' aspects of the role of the public-sector professional. The findings led to the suggestion that while government policies may be contributing to teacher deprofessionalisation, this is not the full story. There also appears to be a failure on the part of schools and teachers to debate and discuss these wider issues of professionalism.

The nature of these findings led to the consideration of the initial training of new entrants to the profession in England and Wales, all the more important now as they are given two-thirds of their training 'on school premises' (DfE 1992). Whilst there are very cogent arguments for the involvement of serving teachers in the initial training of new entrants to the profession, an absence of education in the wider aspects of 'being a professional' is deeply worrying. Teachers, as noted in Chapter 4, are the gate-keepers of a society's traditions, of its culture, as well as being facilitators of development. Teachers, then, more than any other body of professionals, must be intellectually and critically reflective, flexible and adaptable to the changing demands of the young and their society.

With this in mind, an attempt was made to ascertain the attitudes and priorities of mentors in the training they give, as mentors hold the key role in the training of new entrants to the profession. Each student in England and Wales is attached to an experienced teacher in their training school and it is the main responsibility of that mentor to provide the school-based elements of the student's training. So what the mentor communicates, in terms of attitudes, prized knowledge and concepts, may well be crucial not only to the long-term development of such individuals, but to the profession as a whole.

A sample of ninety mentors was drawn from the forty secondary schools that formed a training partnership with a university department of education to provide training for some 200 postgraduate trainees each academic year. The partnership is well established and has been running for a number of years with a very stable membership from its school partners. Only three of the mentors were under 30 years of age, and six over 50 years of age, the vast majority being either between 30 and 40 (33.3%) and between 40 and 50 (56.7%). They also represented a good spread of teaching subject backgrounds. Finally, it is worth noting that the length of teaching career of these mentors again represents a wide spread of experience, with two-thirds having over ten years' experience.

A questionnaire was constructed in order to ascertain mentors' opinions on a range of professional issues which could appear in their initial training work with students. This construction was undertaken using a two-stage process. Rather than construct a questionnaire based just on our values and thinking, and that of the wider academic literature, the validity of the instrument would be significantly enhanced if it incorporated mentors' views. In other words, it was thought desirable for mentors to tell us what they thought were the important points we should consider. To that end an open-ended questionnaire was distributed to a subset of mentors in which they were simply asked to list their views under five 'area' prompts. These were, when dealing with an ITT student:

- What are the main personal and educational qualities needed to be a mentor?
- What do you think are the main tasks of the mentor?
- What do you consider to be the main issues mentors need to tackle?
- What tasks and issues are you more confident in dealing with?
- Which tasks and issues are you less confident in dealing with?

The responses from an initial subset of 30 mentors to these free-response questionnaires were carefully examined and it was quickly apparent that there were a number of recurring themes to which mentors referred. Unsurprisingly, and sensibly, there were many replies that mentioned what could be called matters of classroom technique. For example, classroom management, planning a clear focus for lessons, dealing with special educational needs, and achieving consistency in grading students' teaching competencies were all issues listed by mentors. There were also items in the replies that clearly identified more personal counselling issues, for example, developing relationships with pupils, encouraging a 'professional' approach, taking feedback from students, dealing with deficiencies in students, providing a professional role model, and so on. Now whilst mentors in the subset used the term 'professional', they did so whilst referring to such issues as matters of dress and behaviour. What was lacking in their responses was any reference to the kinds of wider professional issues mentioned earlier. When therefore the main questionnaire instrument was constructed, a number of such issues from the wider literature on teaching, mentoring and initial training were also included. From these sources – the mentors' views, our own research, and the wider academic literature – a list of twenty-four items was then assembled.

The questionnaire itself was designed in four sections. On three two-page spreads, respondents were presented with the same twenty-four items, but in a variety of formats. On the first two-page spread, they were asked about their priorities in terms of the theoretical importance they attached to the items, as if in an 'ideal world' situation. On the second two-page spread, we asked them to prioritise the items in terms of their perception of the actual time they had spent dealing with each item with their first student in the 1996–7 session. On the third two-page spread, we asked mentors to indicate their training priorities/needs against the same twenty-four items. In each of these first three sections the items were presented in a column with three adjacent columns in which respondents were invited to indicate what their priorities were, each column indicating a different level of priority (see an example of this in Table 5.1). The only proviso was that they could not place more than five items in any one column. At the foot of each chart were two single boxes; in one they were asked to identify their top priority item, and in the other their lowest priority item. The last section sought information about the mentors, their age, length of teaching experience, subject, position in the school hierarchy, and the number of students they had mentored since September 1993. After several revisions by the authors, the questionnaire was piloted with a small group of mentors to ensure that the items were understandable and unambiguous. After minor amendments the questionnaire was then issued to the mentors.

The results

In terms of the theoretical importance mentors attached to the questionnaire items, their priorities reveal a clear picture. Table 5.2 gives the percentage frequency of mentors' prioritised responses. What comes across clearly from these data are that mentors believed that their most important tasks were related to matters such as classroom management and planning and providing a clear focus for student lessons. These, when coupled with the importance attached to items that require the development of good relationships with pupils and with getting the best out of pupils, are clearly very commendable; indeed, one would be concerned if those involved in the training process did not lay stress in these areas. That more than 80% of mentors also rated very highly the need to get students to evaluate teaching and to take advice, also shows that as a group, mentors were clearly concerned to ensure that students developed traits that would be vital to them throughout their professional

Table 5.2 Percentages of mentors' stated theoretical priorities attached to key mentoring activities ($n = 90$)

Activity	Most important %	Of some importance %	Least important %
Planning and providing a clear focus for students' lessons	97.8	2.2	0
Discussing the role of teacher unions	1.1	15.6	83.3
Maintaining my students' ideals and enthusiasm	63.3	36.7	0
Helping my students to understand pupil needs	93.3	6.7	0
Getting students to recognise their deficiencies	65.5	33.3	1.1
Discussing the traditions of teaching and schooling	0	22.2	77.8
Putting educational theories into practice	14.4	72.2	13.3
Assessing the students' teaching competencies in each lesson I observe	75.6	23.3	1.1
Discussing the relationship between schools and society	1.1	55.6	43.3
Learning from my student during debriefings	26.7	64.4	8.9
Discussing ethical dilemmas posed by legislation	1.1	27.8	71.1
Focusing on special educational needs	48.9	47.8	3.3
Getting students to evaluate and take advice	94.4	5.6	0
Raising the quality of pupil learning	74.4	25.6	0
Discussing how to maintain the autonomy of the teaching profession	1.1	14.4	84.4
Achieving consistency with the university part of the course	2.2	70.0	27.8
Encouraging working relationships with pupils	81.1	18.9	0
Considering educational theory	1.1	37.8	61.1
Encouraging students to get the best out of pupils	87.8	11.1	1.1
Discussing what makes a professional approach to teaching	11.1	73.3	15.6
Emphasising classroom management	92.2	6.7	1.1
Being consistent in grading students' teaching	20	70	10
Helping students cope with stress and pressure	31.1	62.2	6.7
Appreciating the provisionality of subject knowledge	1.1	33.3	65.6

careers. There should be no complaint about an emphasis on such competences.

It needs to be pointed out that there is a sly seduction in the competences argument because it provides only half an argument. This was eloquently put by J.L. Austin (1970) who coined the phrase 'trouser words' for terms such as 'competence'. In such cases, it is the negative of the word that wears the trousers; naturally no one wants professionals who are incompetent, and therefore the argument goes, we must have competent professionals. This can be achieved, it is naively assumed, through defining what those competencies are and then making them obligatory criteria. The net effect of such a sleight of hand has been neatly summed up by Terry Hyland (1993) when he argued that:

> Programmes based on the functional analysis of work roles are likely to produce teachers who are 'competent' yet ill-equipped for further professional development, uncritical of educational change and largely ignorant of the wider cultural, social and political context in which the role of the teacher needs to be located. Such teachers will be neither experts nor reflective practitioners and, lacking the background provided by education and training approaches based on the concept of professional expertise, will be 'professionals' in name only. (p. 130)

Hyland's prognosis has been shown to have been fulfilled in the results of a number of recent studies. The earlier chapters of this book point in the same direction. Other work by one of the authors (Bottery 1998), in a series of in-depth qualitative studies with serving teachers, found that a great many of his subjects were aware of the educational changes that affected them personally but had little time, and sometimes little interest, in other areas beyond their immediate orbit of concern and were not generally conversant with the wider cultural, social and political context in which the role of the teacher needs to be located. Further, work by Levin and Riffel (1997) in Canada indicates that this is not a national but an international issue, for their research similarly indicates that teachers and school systems are on the whole dominated by conventional wisdom about the purposes and present structures of schools, and see social change as having a negative effect on these present purposes and structures. Instead of actually facing and discussing these problems head on, schools and teachers in the Levin and Riffel study tended to respond through the filters of conventional wisdom, which prevented them from fully appreciating or responding to these changes. As they say (p. 40): '... changes outside the school mattered insofar as they affected what happened in the school'.

The authors therefore saw schools as insufficiently attuned or interested in learning more about such social change and how it should be dealt with; and this, they argued, led to unimaginative and limited strategies in how to adjust and cope with it. The work of Levin and Riffel and the evidence of this book indicate that wider 'ecological' issues do not find any serious place with the priorities of teachers in England and Wales or in Canada, or with mentors in the UK in their training of entrants to the profession.

Examination of Table 5.2 reinforces this conclusion. Thus, when mentors placed in column three of Table 5.2 (those items 'of least importance') items such as 'discussing how to maintain the autonomy of the teaching profession' (84.4%), 'discussing traditions of teaching and schooling' (77.8%), 'discussing ethical dilemmas posed by legislation' (71.1%), and 'discussing the role of teacher unions' (83.3%) it is clear that the overwhelming view of the sample was that these are of little theoretic or practical importance. These results necessarily lead one to question whether the mentors had had the opportunity for such reflection during the course of their professional lives. The question about teacher autonomy received a very low rating from these mentors, and yet one might assume and hope that such autonomy would be viewed as a crucial element of true professionalism.

Similarly, mentor ratings on the importance of the nature of subject knowledge did not fare much better, with nearly two-thirds of the sample saying that 'appreciating the provisionality of our subject knowledge' was among the least important features of their work with trainee teachers. Yet an acquaintance with epistemological and curriculum theory issues would have, one might think, given this a greater centrality. It is conceivable as well that some mentors may not have had the opportunity to consider that the way schools and teaching are presently organised is an accident of history and that this does not have to remain that way.

This possible lack of reflection is supported by Helsby's (1996) survey, reporting that in her interview situations teachers, when asked to provide unprepared answers to questions about professionalism, often gave responses 'off the top of the head', indicating a lack of structured thought on these questions. Helsby's, our results, and those of Levin and Riffel, we suggest, point to a worrying lack of reflection on the deeper and longer-term issues of teacher professionalism. And the danger here is that, rather like frogs used to swimming in water with a slowly rising temperature, teachers may find themselves not only scalded by anti-professional legislation, but perhaps find their professional status boiled away without them realising it.

It could be argued that the responses to the item 'discussing what makes a professional approach to teaching' counter these claims. Two-thirds of our sample indicated that this was of some importance. However, it is useful here to point out the distinction made by Helsby in her research (Helsby 1996). Responses in her sample could be classified, she suggests, in two ways, as 'being a professional' and as 'behaving professionally'. The replies given to our item 'discussing what makes a professional approach to teaching' clearly fall within Helsby's second category, that of behaving professionally. Replies

Table 5.3 Percentages of mentors' stated priorities for use of time with students on mentoring issues (*n* = 90)

Activity	Most important %	Of some importance %	Least important %
Planning and providing a clear focus for students' lessons	93.3	6.7	0
Discussing the role of teacher unions	0	7.8	92.2
Maintaining my students' ideals and enthusiasm	63.3	35.6	1.1
Helping my students to understand pupil needs	87.8	8.9	3.3
Getting students to recognise their deficiencies	70	27.8	2.2
Discussing the traditions of teaching and schooling	0	26.7	73.3
Putting educational theories into practice	10	61.1	28.9
Assessing the students' teaching competencies in each lesson I observe	82.2	15.6	2.2
Discussing the relationship between schools and society	0	40	60
Learning from my student during debriefings	25.6	66.7	7.8
Discussing ethical dilemmas posed by legislation	0	27.8	72.2
Focusing on special educational needs	41.1	55.6	3.3
Getting students to evaluate and take advice	94.4	5.6	0
Raising the quality of pupil learning	67.8	31.1	1.1
Discussing how to maintain the autonomy of the teaching profession	0	10	90
Achieving consistency with the university part of the course	6.7	58.9	34.4
Encouraging working relationships with pupils	77.8	22.2	0
Considering educational theory	0	38.9	61.1
Encouraging students to get the best out of pupils	77.8	21	1.1
Discussing what makes a professional approach to teaching	13.3	66.7	20
Emphasising classroom management	92.2	7.8	0
Being consistent in grading students' teaching	10	82.2	7.8
Helping students cope with stress and pressure	32.2	57.8	10
Appreciating the provisionality of subject knowledge	3.3	47.8	48.9

in our initial open questionnaire such as 'providing a clear role model, being punctual ... setting high personal standards of conduct ... having good interpersonal skills ... being patient ... trust inspiring' give the flavour of the replies. Such behaviour is important but is also very different from having the wider social and 'ecological' understandings and perceptions that are needed for full professionalism, and which are shown to be seriously lacking in the responses of this sample of mentors.

After asking the mentors to indicate the theoretical importance given to the twenty-four items, they were then asked to indicate the priority they had given to these items in terms of time spent discussing them with their students. This, it was felt, would provide an internal check on teachers' responses and also would show whether there were noticeable differences in what teachers said they thought was important and what they felt they had actually done, thus allowing for contingencies related to lack of time for doing a particular task. The results are shown in Table 5.3.

In terms of integrity, the data in Table 5.3 show a high degree of similarity with those given by the sample of mentors for an 'ideal world' situation, and, if it is the case that these are accurate accounts of the time actually spent on these issues, then the points made earlier in this chapter have even more force because the evidence suggests even more strongly that new entrants to the profession have been and are being trained by mentors who not only think that these wider ecological issues are not important, but also that they consistently do not devote time to them nor think that they deserve higher priority in their training provision.

However, despite the strength of the results so far, it is still possible to argue that there are some mentors who feel that they do not spend time on these issues, not because the issues lack importance, but because they feel they lack the expertise to discuss them. Thus, and finally, in case our mentor sample thought that they could not give time or importance to certain areas because they needed further training, education and expertise to do this, we used the third section of the questionnaire to ask them whether they believed they needed further training in these same twenty-four items. The results of this enquiry are presented in Table 5.4.

Of those areas that we would classify as relating to the social and 'ecological' perspective of professional teaching, certainly four of them:

- 'discussing how to maintain the autonomy of the teaching profession'
- 'discussing the relationship between schools and society'
- 'discussing traditions of teaching and schooling'
- 'discussing the role of teacher unions'

were clearly perceived as areas in which a substantial percentage of mentors did not feel they needed further training, confirming their earlier view that these were not of high theoretical importance either. Of the six items in which

Table 5.4 Percentages of mentors indicating priorities for further training needs
(*n* = 90)

Activity	More training welcomed %	More training possibly required %	More training not needed %
Planning and providing a clear focus for students' lessons	41.1	37.8	21.1
Discussing the role of teacher unions	1.1	42.2	56.7
Maintaining my students' ideals and enthusiasm	16.7	71.1	12.2
Helping my students to understand pupil needs	51.1	43.3	5.6
Getting students to recognise their deficiencies	56.7	37.8	5.6
Discussing the traditions of teaching and schooling	1.1	46.7	52.2
Putting educational theories into practice	26.7	60	13.3
Assessing the students' teaching competencies in each lesson I observe	54.4	38.9	6.7
Discussing the relationship between schools and society	4.4	56.7	38.9
Learning from my student during debriefings	15.6	68.9	15.6
Discussing ethical dilemmas posed by legislation	8.9	61.1	30
Focusing on special educational needs	52.2	45.6	2.2
Getting students to evaluate and take advice	56.7	40	3.3
Raising the quality of pupil learning	56.7	40	3.3
Discussing how to maintain the autonomy of the teaching profession	1.1	43.3	55.6
Achieving consistency with the university part of the course	34.4	58.9	6.7
Encouraging working relationships with pupils	30	57.8	12.2
Considering educational theory	12.2	62.2	25.6
Encouraging students to get the best out of pupils	36.7	55.6	7.8
Discussing what makes a professional approach to teaching	8.9	71.1	20
Emphasising classroom management	46.7	42.2	11.1
Being consistent in grading students' teaching	46.7	51.1	2.2
Helping students cope with stress and pressure	23.3	68.9	7.8
Appreciating the provisionality of subject knowledge	2.2	63.3	34.4

just over half the sample indicated they would appreciate more training for their mentor role, two of these items relate to what we would call the interpersonal aspects of mentoring. These items were 'getting students to recognise their deficiencies' and 'getting students to evaluate teaching and take advice'. The other four focus on technical classroom issues, 'special educational needs', 'assessing student competence', 'helping my student understand pupil needs' and 'raising the quality of pupil learning'. None of these would fit naturally into the category of 'ecological issues'.

Conclusions

The conclusions to be drawn from this are very worrying, for they send a very clear picture of the kind of professionalism, or professionalisms, that political authorities, and – it has to be said – teachers, are constructing for the profession. This is probably best understood by examining three different meanings of 'professionalism', and of their applicability to the teaching profession, which Hargreaves and Goodson (1996) describe. One conceptualisation, Classical Professionalism, is seen as an attempt by teachers to model themselves on the legal and medical professions, and, largely because of the different natures of their professional knowledge, does not fit teachers too well. Indeed, Hargreaves and Goodson argue that this attempt by teachers to model themselves too closely upon the classical professionals, may well have led them to embark upon a road of attempted professionalisation rather than of professionalism, and may then have contributed to their present problems by leading them to argue for a status based upon claims that are ultimately unsustainable.

A second form of professionalism, that of Flexible Professionalism, is based, they argue, upon the embedding of practice and expertise within local teacher communities rather than upon scientific certainty, in an attempt to connect more closely with the realities of day-to-day practice. This conception, however, runs the profound risk of fragmenting teachers, and of insulating the local from the influence of the wider picture. Indeed, what has been described in this chapter and in preceding chapters, particularly the consistent lack of emphasis on issues relating to the impact of legislation, the relationship between schools and society and aspects of professional autonomy, may well be partly attributable to this discourse. A desire, then, to connect with local communities, laudable in itself, may actually be a strong contributory factor in preventing teachers from fully appreciating the wider forces impacting upon them. Indeed, as Hargreaves and Goodson say (p. 11), it numbs them '. . . against their capacity to feel committed and to actively engage with bigger social missions of justice, equity and community beyond their own workplace'.

The third form of professionalism described is that of Practical Professionalism, a professionalism located in the practical knowledge and judgement that teachers have of their own work. Drawing heavily on the notion of 'reflective practice', and from the work of Donald Schön (1983), and discussed at some length in Chapter 2, the essence of this professionalism lies in the ability to exercise judgement when situations are full of uncertainty – the 'swampy lowlands' of professional practice. Yet, whilst such insights are useful in describing what professionals actually do, the usefulness of such reflection depends not only on the quality of who is reflecting, but what such individuals actually bring to the reflective process in terms of knowledge content. It has already been argued that an emphasis on knowledge of teaching as a craft may prevent reflection by the teaching profession on the wider ecological issues. This is what Schön tends to suggest in his writing and is also seen in our findings, with their very strong emphasis both on the mentors' theoretical perceptions and on their views of the time devoted to matters such as 'planning a clear focus for lessons, classroom management, understanding pupils' needs and encouraging working relationships with pupils'. When this kind of professionalism is then allied with a false quest for professionalisation, and is joined to the situatedness of flexible professionalism, a recipe is then mixed for the kind of restricted professionalism found in this chapter, and which leads away from the rich (Hargreaves and Goodson would call post-modern) professionalism vital to a truly professional body.

The conclusions to this chapter are strong, unequivocal, and fit with those of preceding chapters. Firstly, it seems clear that the aims of recent educational reforms have been in part to produce 'a strategically planned programme of technical training' (Helsby 1996, p. 135). In so doing, these reforms – and those policy-makers behind them – have begun to create a centrally directed, highly accountable, rigorously inspected teaching force, which is not required to think too much or too deeply about the larger social, moral and political issues, which a richer conception of professionalism would commit them to. As Lawn (1990, p. 389) argued nearly a decade ago:

> Teaching is to be reduced to 'skills', attending planning meetings, supervising others, preparing courses and reviewing the curriculum. It is to be 'managed', to be more 'effective'. In effect the intention is to de-politicize teaching and to turn the teacher into an educational worker ...

Such a teaching profession would not see the need to think for itself, nor to question wider societal trends and forces that impinge directly upon education.

However, and secondly, the conclusion is being reached that this attempt by policy-makers is being supported, whether consciously or unconsciously, by the habits and practices of many in the teaching profession today. The research presented in this chapter, when coupled with the earlier chapters on the provision of professional development education, reinforces a picture in which what appears to be the principal aim of bodies like the United Kingdom Teacher Training Agency – to control and direct the activities and thinking of the teaching profession (Graham 1996) – is increasingly being realised. As initial tutoring, induction and continuing professional development, all the way through to the training of headteachers, are wrapped within a cloak of technical rationality, the TTA may largely succeed in its aims because it appears to be dealing with a teaching profession that is either not aware of, nor sufficiently prepared to debate, its own future.

What can be done about this situation? A first thing is to develop what has already begun in this book – a critique of current developments in the continuing professional development of teachers at the present time, in particular the model of development being structured and implemented by Western developmental agencies like the TTA in England and Wales. Such a critique needs to focus on the limitations of the rationale at the centre of such an approach, which is basically a competency-based approach to teacher training, whilst continuing to set it within wider political perspectives. It also needs to argue that a teaching profession of limited rationality and similarly limited professionalism not only serves controversial political and economic ends. It is also limited in its ability to develop a generation that can adequately respond to the complex and changing demands of a more global environment, as well as to provide the sorts of skills and attitudes required for a more empowered and participative citizenry. This is the task of the next chapter.

6

TOWARDS A NEW VISION OF TRAINING AND INSET

Reflective practice, public and ecological understandings

The data presented in the previous five chapters have provided increasing evidence that the teaching profession has found itself more and more excluded from, and apparently unwilling to participate in, debates about its future; a future increasingly characterised by economic determinism, post-Fordist direction of markets and technical rationalist approaches to professional development couched in terms of reductionist competences. This situation is compounded where those mentors responsible within the profession for the school-based training of new entrants increasingly espouse such views.

In this chapter, an overview of the salient issues influencing the development of the initial and in-service preparation of teachers is presented. It is argued that the characterisation of the present initial and in-service preparation is in an outcomes mode, as suggested in Table 1.1 on page 9. This is limiting for the ultimate purposes of a teaching profession, namely that of an empowering profession whose aims should be to equip its clients (pupils and parents) for a participative, informed and critical role in a democracy, a task rendered all the more crucial in the light of the increasing uncertainties of the global world of the future.

The argument is developed through five main areas. First, it is argued that in seeking to consider the future of the teaching profession, a forward-looking perspective should be adopted, and not, as other critics of education in the past have, through a lament for the passing of a 'golden age'. Second, it will become clear that the key feature in the preparation of teachers over the last couple of decades has been a sharp increase in central control, control of initial preparation, control of in-service preparation and this through an ever more specified range of detailed requirements backed by a punitive inspection regime. Third, in order to measure the attainments of those preparing to become teachers and developing the teaching capabilities of serving teachers, the use of reductionist competences has become the prime vehicle for conceptualising the nature of the skill elements of the preparation for teaching. Fourth, in seeking to develop further the understanding of the preparation of teachers, both initial and in-service, it is argued that the balance between what is termed basic teaching skill preparation and ecological reflective thinking capacities needs to be redressed. Lastly, and most importantly, in this chapter, it is contended that teachers, as members of an empowering profession, must themselves be capable of thinking; thinking critically, imaginatively and proactively, of not merely coping with change but of unleashing creativity to meet the challenges of living with uncertainty.

Looking forwards

In Chapter 1, a complex argument was presented, which sought to derive out of an historical context an understanding of the policy issues and dilemmas that face governments at the end of the twentieth century. One key element that underpins much of the thinking of those policy-makers is economic. Since the oil crises of the 1970s, Western governments have been increasingly dogged by two lines of thinking; one focuses on the finite nature of resources, and in particular financial provision, and the second is characterised by a reductionist, linear argument, in which there is an assumed (but unproven) link between schooling and economic performance. In combination, these two have had a serious and restricting effect on the development of education policy. Whilst the first argument sets the context, and it would be folly to argue that material resources are infinite, it is the way that the second argument comes into play that has bedevilled much educational thinking. Because the first argument points to the limited nature of financial and material resources, there has developed a notion of 'national need'. This idea has assumed increasingly important proportions during the last two decades of the twentieth century and is the real shibboleth that has come to 'dog' policy thinking about 'futures' in education. The increased prominence of the idea can be seen through the following extracts from Western policy pronouncements of the last twenty years.

Looking across the Atlantic to the USA, the publication in 1983 of *A Nation at Risk* by the National Commission for Excellence in Education issued stark warnings. An assumed rising tide of mediocrity was declared to be:

an act of unthinking, unilateral educational disarmament

the danger of which was that:

Our once unchallenged pre-eminence in commerce, industry, science and technical innovation is being overtaken by competitors throughout the world.

These sentiments were echoed by Bill Clinton from Arkansas in 1986:

We have watched our jobs in the manufacture of shoes, clothes, textiles, electric motors and rubber products disappear or move overseas. ... Arkansans have noted what many other leaders in the South have noted: that the key to economic growth is a strong education system. (Clinton 1986, p. 28)

In Australia, developments during the 1980s and into the 1990s were underpinned by the same economic agenda as this statement from the Ebbeck Report (1990) demonstrates:

Underpinning the new policies is the necessity to achieve a strong economic base for Australia. ... To this end, the Government affirmed its intention that an increased share of total higher education resources should be directed to those fields of study of greatest relevance to the national goals of industrial development and economic restructuring. (pp. 7–8)

In the United Kingdom, Prime Minister James Callaghan's Ruskin speech, delivered in 1976, reflected growing evidence of the increasing interests and concerns of policy-makers with this issue.

With the increasing complexity of modern life, we cannot be satisfied with maintaining existing standards, let alone observe any decline. ... To the teachers I would say that you must satisfy the parents and industry that what you are doing meets their requirements and the needs of our children. (James Callaghan, speech at Ruskin College, Oxford, October 1976, quoted in Chitty 1989, pp. 93–4)

In *Better Schools* of 1985 the then UK Conservative Government was clearly exercised by the idea as it stated:

The quality of school education concerns everyone. What is achieved by those who provide it, and by the pupils for whom it is provided, has lasting effects on the prosperity and well being of each individual citizen and of the whole nation. ... Britain's place in the world has changed and our membership of the European Community is increasingly influencing our society and our economic opportunities. (DES 1985, paras 1 and 3)

The consultation paper on the UK National Curriculum in 1987 gave the lie when it stated:

We must raise standards consistently, at least as quickly as they are rising in competitor countries. (para. 6)

New Labour's first major policy statement, *Excellence in Schools*, continues the theme:

> We are talking about investing in human capital in the age of knowledge. To compete in the global economy, to live in a civilised society and to develop the talents of each and every one of us, we will have to unlock the potential of every young person. (DfEE 1997, p. 3)

These extracts amply make the point that, for the last two decades, this idea of 'national need' has been prevalent behind much key educational policy thinking around the Western world and across party political divides. As long ago as 1981, Dearden commented that:

> 'National need' [is] a notion as imprecise as it is thought to be important. (p. 107)

and went on to draw out the implications of this in the following terms; it is:

> an educationally disastrous mistake, to infer from the premise that society needs x the conclusion that therefore everyone must learn x, whether x is engineering science, electronics or French. (pp. 116–17)

This is the danger that arises from the acceptance of the second argument and the value positions upon which it is based. When an educational problem or issue is identified, all too often a 'solution' is considered that is predicated upon a facile acceptance that there exists a linear, often causal relationship between the problem and the proposed solution. The argument then proceeds in a simplistic and reductionist manner. The assumption is that the future is in some ways predictable and controllable; if certain things are done, certain policy initiatives are started, then particular outcomes will happen. For example, if schools are required to have a policy on sex education, this should help reduce teenage pregnancies. Schools, in England and Wales, were required to have such policies as part of the 1986 Education Act, but most recent statistics for the later 1990s show a marked increase in the numbers of such pregnancies. Now it could be argued that perhaps there should have been more policies to deal with this problem or that those that were developed were of an inappropriate kind. If that were the case, then it points even more strongly to the present argument, namely, that in this situation which is complex, there are other variables at work and that therefore a neat, simple solution is misguided.

In the 1993 review of the National Curriculum in England and Wales, the assumed link between economic performance, educational standards and 'national need' provided a driving rationale.

In a highly competitive world there is nowhere to hide. The fact that standards of educational achievement are rising internationally, and in particular, in the Far East, means that our future as a nation depends upon the improvements we can make to our education system. (Dearing 1994, para. 3.1)

It is remarkable how these worries expressed by Dearing (1994) identify the perceived dangers of economic competition from the Pacific Rim. Yet by 1998, the Western world was fraught with worry, not that the Pacific Rim was going to overcome Western economies by its competitive edge but that its potential collapse was going to prove more serious, engulfing the West through failure rather than success. The mistake is to fall for an assumed linearity of argument. Hargreaves (1994) sums the problem up succinctly:

Reform is often guided by the belief that every problem has a solution. Perhaps the real challenge of reform as a continuous process, though, is acknowledging that every solution has a problem. (p. 138)

The future is not going to unfold in a neat, linear and solvable form.

An instructive and illustrative example of this is for the reader to undertake the following exercise. The requirement is to consider oneself as living at the turn of the nineteenth century. The problem is predicting what the key educational needs of society will be in the new century (i.e. the twentieth century). There is, in this example, an obvious intrusion of hindsight from a position at the end of the twentieth century. Yet even trying to think in terms of the main preoccupations of those at the end of the nineteenth century in, for example, England, one would have a great, if not impossible task. The advances that were made during the first twenty years of the century in fields such as flight, the mass production of the motor car, the increased role for women in society, the development of the destructive capacity of weapons and the medical advances were, to say the least, substantial. What were the educational implications of these developments, and how should policy-makers and planners have prepared for them at the turn of the previous century?

At the turn of the twentieth century, the problem is similar. What writers in other areas are pointing to are issues such as being 'beyond certainty' (Handy 1995), living in a chaotic world, of the need for 'learning organisations' (Garratt 1990, Senge 1990, Holly 1990), of organisations that are like 'moving mosaics' (Toffler 1991), of the need to develop 'insights', 'creativity' and 'artistry' (West-Burnham 1997) in approaches to life, learning and work. It is a delusion to succumb to a linear approach to thinking about such matters. Instead, educationists might do well to recognise Hargreaves' vision of:

... a post modern world characterised by flexibility, adaptability, creativity, opportunism, collaboration, continuous improvement and a positive orientation towards problem solving. (Hargreaves 1994, p. 63)

It is lessons in these that are needed from the business world much more than the mechanics of the market or the use of a business lexicon in schools.

At the present time, when coping with rapid change in continuous preparation for an unclear future is on everyone's agenda, commercial organisations have taken the idea of the learning organisation as a response to the need for rapid organisational development and so their focus is away from narrow issues of control to the wider field of learning. Garratt (1987) observes that for an organisation to survive and develop, the rate of learning within the organisation must be equal to or greater than the rate of change in the external environment.

It is worth remembering that any organisation is essentially a collection of individuals joined together in pursuit of common goals. Thus schools, which are organisations, must also be seen as constituted of individuals. If Garratt's dictum is true for organisations, then it follows that it must equally apply to the organisation's individual members. The key questions then become ones of learning and control. The worrying irony here is that, in the experience in England, schools are being forced to do just the opposite from the practices of the commercial world. There is more control through Ofsted inspections than ever before; there is more control through the stipulation of teaching 'standards' by the Teacher Training Agency; and there is more control and accountability through testing, National Curriculum tests and published 'league tables'. After such a litany of control, one would be well justified in asking where the learning aspect of this equation has gone. Learning constitutes the more important side of the equation and in schools, whose assumed task is the preparation of the next generation, it should not be unreasonable to expect those who work there to be encouraged to 'practise what they preach'. The lamentable situation is that for professionals in schools, opportunities for more open-ended, critical, creative and proactive thinking have been expunged from initial training and almost eradicated from most provision of in-service work for serving professionals. The next section will demonstrate that initial and in-service preparation of teachers has been forced to conform to an agenda predicated upon increased control and accountability and an almost total curtailment of opportunity for innovation, experiment and learning (as opposed to training) for professionals.

Increased control of teacher preparation

Taking as a case study developments in England and Wales, the key feature of the last three decades of teacher preparation has been the change from a

106

situation of very little central control to one of imposed central control. This can be seen clearly in Table 1.2 (on page 12) where in the period of social democracy, there were no government standards, yet by the phase of the New Modernisers, there are now strict, rigorous and ever-expanding government standards. The turning points in the development of the agendas for both initial preparation and for in-service preparation came with two circulars in the mid-1980s, *Circular 3/84* (DES 1984) which introduced the first elements of control in the initial preparation of teachers and *Circular 6/86* (DES 1986) which brought about a sea change in in-service arrangements for serving teachers. The purpose of this section is to trace these developments, showing how they reflect the policy developments outlined in Chapter 1, first with the case of initial preparation and then subsequently with in-service provision.

At the height of the period of social democracy, in the early 1970s, the James report (DES 1972) in its summary for initial preparation did not specify more than in this statement about the requirements of the content of a teacher-training programme:

> The first year would normally be in a professional institution, whether a college education or the education department of a university or polytechnic, and would cover both the theoretical exploration of disciplines contributing to the study of education, and practical work. The training would be specifically related to the teacher's prospective needs in his first appointment. ... At the end of the first year, successful students would be recommended to the Secretary of State for recognition as 'licensed teachers' and would proceed to the second year of the cycle, which would consist of largely school-based training. (DES 1972, para. 6.10)

At this time, training was conducted in colleges of education, education departments in polytechnics and education departments in universities. The training curriculum was a matter for the academic staff in these institutions and the decision to award the qualifications at the end of the courses was similarly reserved to the higher-education institution. Notable by absence in this process was any form of central stipulation and equally, from the other end of the spectrum, of any formal involvement of teachers. Such an approach could be said to represent the high-water mark of a *laissez-faire* attitude to teacher preparation yet is not consonant with the argument developed through this book of teaching as an empowering profession. Such a profession is almost certainly better developed by means of a centrally devised framework (not a strait-jacket), a partnership between practitioners, researchers and theorists and a regulatory framework provided through a general teaching council for three reasons. First, a framework should ensure common baseline standards of acceptability; provide the basis for the assurance of quality yet be flexible enough to permit and encourage initiative, innovation and development. Second, the development of partnerships is a necessity for the creative development of responsive, adaptable, research-based approaches to developing better learning and teaching. Third, a regulatory framework provided by such as a general teaching council would oversee standards on entry, monitor professional development and ensure adherence to ethical standards of practice.

With the advent of a Conservative government after 1979, a severe economic recession in the early 1980s and the need to challenge and up-date many practices in the country, the then Secretary of State, Sir Keith Joseph, issued a White Paper, *Teaching Quality* (DES 1983) in 1983. At this time there had been significant challenges to the position of trades unions within the body politic. Given that many union leaders at this time perceived changes in union legislation as restrictive, it was felt that the proposals contained in *Teaching Quality* represented something of a threat. No amount of extensive references within the paper to the need to improve the 'match' between teachers, their abilities, skills, knowledge and expertise and what the school and the curriculum demanded of them could hide the content of para. 81.

> Concern for quality demands that in the small minority of cases where, despite in-service training arrangements, teachers fail to maintain a satisfactory standard of performance, employers must, in the interests of pupils, be ready to use procedures for dismissal. (DES 1983, p. 25)

This was linked to the pronouncements of the Secretary of State on the subject of teacher assessment:

> I attach particular importance to the interesting and innovative work ... in the important area of teacher assessment. (Sir Keith Joseph, speech to North of England Conference, Jan. 1984)

and on his stated desire to remove incompetent teachers from the classroom.

Against this background, and explicitly presaged in para. 106 of *Teaching Quality*, the Secretary of State introduced *Circular 3/84* (DES 1984) which for the first time established the Secretary of State's criteria for the award of qualified teacher status, made stipulations about the nature of teacher-training programmes and length of time to be served in schools and established a monitoring council, the Council for the Accreditation of Teacher Education (CATE) under the chairmanship of Sir William Taylor. Furthermore, as a condition of accreditation, university departments were to be subject to inspection by HMI and university tutors involved with pedagogy would 'need to demonstrate their effectiveness in schools' (DES 1984, annex para. 4).

Control by central government was further tightened five years later with another circular, 24/89, which placed particular stress on aspects of course content and specified precise criteria. The hitherto one-sided control of teacher education by the universities was again challenged in 1992 with the development of partnership requirements whereby schools were to take a leading role in the training arrangements, including the planning of courses and the delivery of parts of the programmes. In this way, the necessary contributions of practitioners were now to be formally required in the training processes. Universities were to provide financial recompense to schools for their new, formal involvement in the training process without additional recurrent expenditure to meet what were considered as additional costs. Here the instigation of a market mechanism was deliberately used as a ploy to weaken further the control of the universities in the direction of teacher education (Wright 1993). The process of wresting control of teacher education from universities and colleges was completed with the establishment of the Teacher Training Agency (TTA) in 1994. This agency set about its task using the principles of 'new managerialism' and sought, through the use of ever more detailed criteria and inspection by Ofsted, to assert its complete control of the teacher-training agenda. The advent of the Blair government has seen the continuation of this line of policy. *Circular 4/98* provides the most detailed stipulations for teacher training. Gone are the broad statements of principle found in 3/84, whilst the competence statements of 9/92 have been dressed in the shining armour of 'standards', ready to transform teachers into the most regulated set of public-service technicians.

The following extracts from these circulars, 3/84, 9/92 and 4/98, are given here because the increasing level of detail in the prescription is instructive, and further supports the contention expressed in Figure 1.2 that there is a much increased emphasis on 'steering'. This is *Circular 3/84*:

> Courses should give adequate attention to the methodology of teaching the chosen subject specialism ... the approach to teaching method should differentiate according to the age group which the student intends to teach while giving due emphasis to the differences between children in the rates at which they develop and learn. (DES 1984, annex para. 8).

Circular 9/92 was couched in terms of 'competences'. These were broad statements each covering in no more than a short paragraph or two the areas of subject knowledge, subject application, class management, assessment and recording of pupils' progress and further professional development.

Circular 4/98, however, announced itself in the following way:

> The standards set out in this document replace the more general 'competences' set out in DFE Circulars 9/92 and 14/93...

There then follows almost ten pages of detailed prescription.

These standards are then reinforced by a published *National Curriculum for Initial Teacher Training* in which even more prescription is given. This is an extract from the section for Primary English:

> 3b that in order to enable pupils to read, write and spell individual words, they must teach pupils:
>
> (i) to recognise and be able to write the letters (graphemes) that represent the initial dominant sounds;
>
> (ii) to hear, identify and blend phonemes into words;
>
> (iii) to identify the phonemes in words and segment words into their constituent sounds;
>
> (iv) that phonemes may be represented by different graphemes e.g. pl<u>ay</u>, pl<u>a</u>c<u>e</u>, r<u>ai</u>n, w<u>eigh</u>, and know the range of spellings that can represent a single vowel sound;
>
> (v) to recognise patterns of spelling related to word families, letter strings and derivations;
>
> (vi) to distinguish syllabic boundaries and use this skill to build up multi-syllabic words in the reading and segment words for spelling.
>
> (DfEE 1998, pp. 35–6)

The TTA indicate that all providers of training will be subject to inspection by Ofsted and that unsatisfactory grades in key cells of the inspection matrix can lead to steps to withdraw the provider's accreditation, as evidenced in the *Times Educational Supplement* (1998, p. 2) or by some major providers withdrawing from phases of teacher training altogether.

Besides the clear increase in central control, described as 'the racheting up of toughness' (Moon 1998, p. 30) other issues emerge from this overview of the development of initial training. Three are related. The first concerns the increased marginalisation of the input by higher education institutions. The second is the implication of the increased responsibility given to teachers as part of the training process, and the third is the reduced capacity for innovation within the system.

It can be argued that the first of these, the marginalisation of the role of higher-education institutions, represents a reduction of the 'theoretical' content of programmes. In the context of England and Wales this could be seen as an indulgence in that peculiarly British dislike of theory. As part of the preparation for teachers, those who are expected to lead the young and the new generations into the uncertain world of the twenty-first century, such attempts to reduce the requirements on such people to think for themselves, to show insight and creativity and to demonstrate these skills to their charges, seems remarkably myopic. This approach stands in contrast to the development, for example, in France of the IUFM (Instituts Universitaires de Formation des Maîtres), where students are involved in a two-year programme comprising a first year within the IUFM following a range of educational courses and a second year where there is continuous involvement with a school. The programme requires the production of a 'mémoire professionnel', a professional dissertation which is aimed at promoting a critical and evaluative approach to practice.

The second issue, that greater formal responsibilities have been given to teachers in the training process, is of a Janus-like nature. One aspect concerns the important 'practical' aspects of teacher preparation. This is recognised through the formal involvement of serving teachers, the increase in the time required to be served on school premises, and the undeniably practical aspects of the 'standards' by which students are to be assessed. The other aspect of the formal involvement of teachers relates to teachers' self-perceptions and the socialisation processes of teachers. This is a more serious concern. Teachers, who for years have been the butt of a 'discourse of derision' (Ball 1990, p. 22), who themselves have suffered innovation overload since the late 1980s and feel increasingly alienated from the work and vocation they came into, are now charged with very significant responsibilities in the training of new entrants to teaching. What has been systematically taken away from teachers has been the need for them to think creatively about key curriculum decisions. They have been transformed into the empowered implementers of the policy decisions of others. The post-Fordist policies of the late 1980s and early 1990s transformed schools and their teachers into something of a giant educational Panopticon (Sewell and Wilkinson 1992) where the gaoler is Ofsted. Teachers, for whom a key task has always been the socialisation of pupils into schools and the compliance culture necessary for the smooth operation of such organisations, now find themselves set up to induct new trainees into the same compliance culture where requirements are dictated from the centre and conformity is checked by the Ofsted inspector. Such a system leads directly to the third criticism, namely the reluctance of parts of the system to innovate for itself.

It has been increasingly difficult in the English context to gain the sustained involvement of schools and training institutions in innovative projects often because of the twin drivers of heavy central control occasioning fear and time pressure, and a growing teacher compliance culture. In less regulated contexts, schools are more keen to join in with innovative projects relating to aspects of the curriculum or to developing approaches to learning; for example the 'Saxophone Project' (no date), which has sought to use new communications technologies to develop collaborative real-time working projects with schools in North America and Europe. In teacher development, such projects offer schools and their pupils real opportunities which are often possible only through the involvement of a higher-education institution where there may be access to advanced technologies. Projects such as these have also provided stimulating experiences for trainee teachers. The dangers of the present authoritarian approach to teacher education in England and the emerging teacher culture is that this is less and less of a possibility; innovation is not on the agenda.

> At the present time we are struggling with over-specified curricula and a rigid and reactionary assessment framework for teacher education. If higher education and schools in partnership are to take best advantage of the shared intellectual and physical resources, then they must have more freedom to innovate with the curriculum. (O'Shea 1997)

A similar pattern of intervention, control and more control can be seen in the arrangements for the in-service development of teachers in England. The nature of the arrangements have changed from one in the late 1970s where there was very significant freedom for teachers to determine their professional development, to participate in long award-bearing courses offered in higher-education institutions, to a system of ever-increasing regulation, prescription and inspection, evidenced by the publication of national standards for headteachers, subject leaders, *SENCOS* (Special Educational Needs Co-ordinators), and newly qualified teachers (DfEE 1998), an inspection framework (Ofsted 1995) and a funding mechanism which is based on the outcomes of the inspection process.

The changes in in-service provision can be traced back to *Circular 6/86* (DES 1986) where, for the first time, national training priorities were identified. Since then there has been a continuous process of linking training priorities ever more closely to the agenda first of the National Curriculum and then to matters relating to literacy, numeracy, information and communication technologies (ICT) competence and the raising of standards. What this has served to achieve is the development of a group of public-service technicians. That this provision is repeatedly referred to as 'training' underlines further the linear approach to developing policy described earlier in this chapter. The idea is that in pursuit of satisfying 'national need', 'reform' programmes, such as in the National Curriculum and all the associated developments, teachers are in deficit and need to be equipped to deliver the new programmes. The programmes themselves have particular implementational requirements and it is for these fixed objectives that teachers are then trained. Training may be an appropriate approach where the ends of the programme are fairly clear but the contention here is that this is first at one remove from where teachers should be operating, and second that in terms of the uncertain future to which reference has been made earlier, closed training is far from appropriate. Teachers, faced with massive degrees of innovation, have been the recipients of 'just-in-time training', where the provision of time to reflect, to think and to be critical has been expunged from the process. Teachers and teaching are impoverished as a result.

Teaching, competences and standards

Since the 1980s the questions of assessing teaching, of defining unacceptable practice, have been on the political agenda. In the United States, Bill and Hilary Clinton started the process in Arkansas with the Arkansas Educational Skills Assessment Test. As Bill Clinton put it:

> We were the first state to require our existing, already certificated teachers and administrators to pass a basic skills exam in order to be recertified. . . . Having raised the sales tax to increase teacher pay, we felt we ought to assure an appropriate level of basic competency. (Clinton 1986, p. 29)

In England, the process for ensuring greater competence of teachers began with the publication of *Teaching Quality* (DES 1983). In pursuit of the goal of improving teaching, there has been a resurgence in the use of competence-based approaches. Such an approach lends itself to bureaucratic rationalisation, to goal-reduction strategies, expressed by Wise (1979) in the following terms:

> In the past policy makers were content to render goals for education abstractly, globally, and with the highest expectations rhetoric could muster. Goals stated in such terms were not only difficult to put into operation – they were perhaps unattainable altogether. Policy makers now prefer goals which appear attainable and which are measurable. (p. 29)

The aptness of these views is well exemplified in the extracts quoted earlier in this chapter from circulars 3/84 (DES 1984), 9/92 (DfE 1992) and 4/98 (DfEE 1998). Add to this Moon's gloss on bureaucratic rationalisation, a process whereby bureaucratic activity increases to ensure that practices conform to norms (Moon 1998), and the problems associated with incompetent teachers identified in the 1980s by politicians, one can see why what Moon calls a 'first order solution' is so attractive to policy makers. A 'first order solution' is, he says, 'the creation of a programme with the same name as the problem, thereby giving the public the impression that the dilemma is being dealt with' (Moon 1998, p. 12).

So, if the problem is dealing with a suspected lack of 'competence' on the part of teachers as suggested in England, the way forward is to create a policy of developing competence.

If the problem was seen, as in the United States, as needing '. . . active leadership in the redesign of schools and in helping their colleagues to uphold high standards of learning and teaching' (Carnegie Forum 1986, p. 55), then a policy of creating 'lead teachers' would be part of the rhetoric involved in this solution.

Returning to England, if the problem has been one of recruiting and retaining teachers where the cause is perceived as the low status of the teaching profession, then the response has been to initiate a policy entitled 'Teaching: high status, high standards' (DfEE 1998). So, if the policy rationale for pursuing a competency-based approach to teacher preparation can be explained in terms of the recent argument, how is this worked out in practice and with what implication?

Reductionism, competence and teaching

The classical way in which competences are derived is through a process of goal reductionism, atomisation and then goal specification (see Jessup 1995). A particular task, work performance or activity will be scrutinised and then deconstructed into what are perceived to be its constituent parts. These can be said to form the steps involved in the overall process or activity. It then is a matter of establishing a sense of progression through the various sub-tasks or activities which together will constitute the whole task. The objective for the trainee is to complete satisfactorily each of the steps, the underlying assumption being that at the end, if all have been accomplished satisfactorily, then the outcome will be a competent performer. Put in these terms, the argument is seductively simple, a policy-maker's ideal solution to the original problem. Hyland, however, suggests that 'One of the attractions of competence is that it has an objective ring to it and carries with it the idea of rigorous adherence to agreed standards' (Hyland 1990, p. 18). As with all neat and simple solutions to complex problems, in this case with the subject of the constituent parts of the processes of teaching, it is all too easy to succumb. The real seriousness of this situation is exacerbated when the competence approach is elevated to panacea proportions and exalted as '*the* singular educational discourse' (emphasis in original, Smyth and Shacklock 1998).

There appear to be four assumptions contained within the current hegemony of 'competences':

1   The first assumption is that measurable assessment can form the basis of the development of more effective teachers.
2   The second assumption is, in the case of complex human interactions like teaching, that 'the sum of the parts equals the whole'.
3   The third is that competences can bring about the assessment of all aspects of a complex social and moral activity such as teaching.
4   The fourth assumption is that competence statements can give an objectivity through defining performance criteria.

The competence approach, it is argued, leads to deficiencies, inadequacies, a lack of moral foundation, a spurious objectivity and produces a terminal 'pathologenic' state (Moore 1996), giving rise to outcomes worse than those original problems which the policy was designed to obviate. Each assumption will be considered in turn.

Assumption one: measurable assessments can form the basis of the development of more effective teachers

It is easy to see why, in a context where policy-makers have been concerned with a perceived lack of performance on the part of teachers, an approach based on competences would be not only politically astute, enabling them to be seen to be doing something, but also providing a means to measure to what extent progress along their agenda was being made.

There is, in the literature on competences, a recognisable division of approaches into those that focus increasingly on more and more specific statements and others that have tended to move towards 'generic' competences. (See Norris 1991, Elliott 1989, MacDonald *et al.* 1987.) In the arena of teaching, the early competence statements as evidenced in *Circular 9/92* (DfE 1992) seemed to have been developing along more 'generic' lines. It has been found, however, in attempts to operationalise these statements, that there was considerable scope for varied interpretation and calls from practising teacher mentors for 'descriptors' of aspects of classroom practice. As a result of this and as a consequence of a desire on the part of the TTA to be more 'hard-nosed' in assessing competences demonstrated by student teachers, the more recent expressions of competence statements veer ever more towards greater specificity, for example:

> ... those to be awarded Qualified Teacher Status should, when assessed, demonstrate that they:
> (a) have a working knowledge and understanding of:
> (i) teachers' professional duties as set out in the current School Teachers' Pay and Conditions document, issued under the School Teachers' Pay and Conditions Act 1991;
> (ii) teachers' legal liabilities and responsibilities relating to:
>   * the Race Relations Act 1976;
>   * the Sex Discrimination Act 1975;
>   * Section 7 and Section 8 of the Health and Safety at Work, etc. Act 1974;
>   * teachers' common-law duty to ensure that pupils are healthy and safe on school presmises and when leading activities off the school site, such as educational visits, school outings or field trips;
>   * what is reasonable for the purposes of safeguarding or promoting children's welfare (Section 3(5) of the Children Act 1989);
>   * the role of the education service in protecting children from abuse (currently set out in DfEE Circular 10/95 and the

Home Office, Department of Health, DfEE and Welsh Office
Guidance *Working Together: a guide to arrangements for
inter-agency co-operation for the protection of children from
abuse* 1991);
- appropriate physical contact with pupils (currently set out in
DfEE Circular 10/95);
- appropriate physical restraint of pupils (Section 4 of the
Education Act 1997 and DfEE Circular 9/94);
- the detention of pupils on disciplinary grounds (Section 5 of
the Education Act 1997). (DfEE 1998).

Both the specific and the generic approaches to competence present serious
problems. In their 'generic' form, the statements give an air of 'spurious
precision' (Norris 1991) and so fail to give the sought-for clarity and
uniformity about ends or outcomes. In the greater specification of detail as
evidenced in *Circular 4/98* (DfEE 1998), a path towards the absurd is being
beaten. At what point will there be sufficient precision and detail in the
statements for assessors to be able to assert unequivocally that competences
are being displayed and in the present jargon, 'standards' are being met or
bettered? The level of detail in the above prescription exemplifies the situation
that regulation has reached the point of simply being silly.

The evidence already cited from UK education circulars clearly exemplifies
a trend towards greater specificity of competence statements and an increased
desire through inspection processes to measure outcomes and hence satisfy
accountability criteria. The inspection data are then to be used to inform
funding lines and allocations of student numbers and to exert policy steers
(TTA 1996). In these terms it should now be clear that the purpose of
competences is one of accountability through measurement.

> It cannot be stressed too often that competence strategies are
> concerned only with measurement, assessment and accreditation, not
> with learning and education *per se*. (Hyland 1993, p. 60)

If this is the case, how can measurable assessments facilitate the development
of more effective teachers? When things begin to go wrong in a classroom, for
some, using a list of competences takes on the proportions of an
insurmountable inventory of demands. Moore (1996) described this situation
as the 'pathologisation of the individual' which she explains in the following
way. The competences list 'becomes a rod with which the teacher beats her
own back'. As put by one teacher: 'These are the things I'm told I have to do.
I'm doing them, but things are still going wrong; therefore I can't be doing
them properly' (p. 206). When this approach is used with serving teachers it is
easy to see why morale is plummeting, self-esteem falling and teaching looks
an unattractive proposition. The danger here lies in the assumption that the

competences approach with its reductive tendencies has a monopoly of rectitude. Teaching, and learning for that matter, are far more complex, multi-faceted issues than a competence approach would concede. In such circumstances, the approach would have the opposite outcome from the original intention; instead of making the teaching more effective, failure is compounded. When competence is seen as the sole approach for professional preparation, rather than as one of many which should be open to critique, discussion and refinement, such a single-track approach is not only dangerously myopic but also immoral.

In the light of what was said earlier about organisations needing to deal with the key issues of learning and control, the adoption of a competence model presents a real danger of taking the development of teachers down a route diametrically opposed to one that is likely to be a key development for education of both teachers and their students for life in the uncertainties of the twenty-first century.

Assumption two: the sum of the parts equals the whole

Competences are a species of behavioural objectives, one criticism of which is that they can lead to trivialisation.

> Trivial learning behaviours are the easiest to operationalise, hence the really important outcomes of education will be under-emphasised. (Stenhouse 1975, p. 72)

The dangers here are that those aspects that can be readily observed and assessed will tend to assume greater prominence than they really warrant and that other areas, which may be less susceptible to ready assessment, will drop from the picture. The net result is that in dividing the whole into competences in the first place, a 'full picture' was never there in the beginning and with time, aspects that prove to be more difficult to assess will tend to atrophy, reducing even further the whole. Cairns (1992), writing from an Australian perspective, argues that a competence model inevitably fails to recognise the complex interactions that constitute effective teaching, and by focusing on checklists of pre-determined criteria, also fails to address or value more 'elusive' attributes to successful teaching and learning such as creativity, initiative, flexibility of decision-making and open-ended outcomes.

This reduces to an ever more mechanistic, limited and limiting approach. Victims of this are the relational aspects of teaching which are difficult to specify in competence descriptors. Yet it is aspects such as developing positive relationships with pupils and colleagues, omitted from the statements contained in *Circular 9/92* (DfE 1992), that are so important. Supporters of competences might argue at this point that developing positive relationships is a competence statement. Such a statement would not help a trainee to know how to develop towards such a situation and the tricky, if not futile task of trying to deconstruct such an end-state into its constituent developmental parts probably explains why such difficult, elusive attributes are omitted.

Assumption three: competences can bring about the assessment of all aspects of a complex social and moral activity such as teaching

Early statements of competence in teacher education in England and Wales as evidenced in *Circular 9/92* (DfE 1992) focused in general terms on broad areas of teaching activity such as subject knowledge, subject application, classroom management, special educational needs, assessment of pupils and so on. Of concern to many teacher educators was the absence of consideration of the relational aspects of teaching; of the need for the development of good relationships both with pupils and colleagues. The social context of relationships is surely crucial. Some student teachers blossom in certain conditions, under the guidance of a particular mentor, yet in other contexts they look quite 'incompetent'. The pre-specification of competence statements leads many trainee teachers to consider the process as one of having to jump through the correct sequence and number of hoops; there is a mechanistic approach to developing their abilities as teachers. Where do such matters as creativity, imagination, ingenuity and other unorthodoxies fit?

More recent statements, for example some of those dealing with ICT include the phrase 'as appropriate' where the apparent intention of the authors of the competence statement implies a technological or pedagogical solution. What this fails to provide is any moral foundation for making decisions, for example about the acceptance or rejection of particular content that might be found by pupils on the Internet, or how trainee teachers should help pupils to develop a responsible attitude to searching on the Internet.

Trying to express the totality of the social, relational, moral and personal aspects of teaching in competence statements leads to a narrow, mechanistic, instrumental, amoral and wholly inadequate view of what is encompassed in the processes of teaching.

Assumption four: competence statements can give an objectivity through defining performance criteria

As has already been mentioned, competences suggest a 'spurious precision' (Norris 1991, p. 334). What needs to be borne in mind is that in the very process of creating the statement of competence, the task or aspect of performance has been deconstructed into what are thought by the authors of the deconstruction to be the appropriate constituent parts. These are then passed on to those whose competence is to be assessed, both assessors and students. There is then contained within the process an assumption that when the parts are reconstructed, there is but one way to reassemble them. That is one fallacy.

The second fallacy is that in terms of discourses, that of the creators of the statements is the same as that of those who are the users of the statements. In the UK Moore (1996) reported that beginning teachers experienced considerable difficulty with competences as a 'universal blueprint' for teaching and with the manner in which it excluded consideration of the 'idiosyncratic, contingent elements of classroom practice'. Crucially, they encountered difficulties in the way competences presented themselves as 'fundamentally fixed and unchallengeable, ... appear[ing] as products of the collective, disinterested wisdom of "other people"' (Moore 1996, p. 204).

In commenting on the Advanced Skills Teacher scheme from Australia, Smyth and Shacklock (1998) present detailed evidence to demonstrate that the discourse of teachers preparing their applications for the scheme are not those of the authors of the criteria. Many teachers, commended by their peers for their classroom performance, found their applications for AST unsuccessful, because they had not articulated the policy assimilations that were required. 'The discursive borders of the skill discourse describe a pedagogical terrain which favours those teachers who are prepared to be proselytised to new policy and school reform by becoming school-site conduits for the latest educational ideology' (Smyth and Shacklock 1998, p. 187). With such misalignments of discourses it is difficult to see how competence statements can provide objectivity. Clearly, for any users of competence statements, the perceptions of teaching by those who practise it are not the same as those administrators who write competence statements about it.

The four assumptions which have been examined strongly point to a conclusion that competency-based approaches *per se* are inappropriate as the sole style or route for teacher preparation. That is not an argument that teachers do not need basic skills or that these should not form part of their initial and continuing preparation. It has been consistently argued throughout this book that teaching is a complex, multi-faceted and moral activity. To foster such development needs more than mere competences. It is to other aspects of this argument that the following sections refer.

On the need to balance skill and reflection

During the last decade or so, teachers have had to cope with a deluge of innovation in terms of curriculum, management, and an assault on the fundamental principles of schooling which have been significantly changed as a result of economic rationalist arguments. At the same time, schools have been faced with considerable social changes and teachers find that they are having to deal with many ensuing issues, for example, inclusive schooling and communications technologies. These and others like them represent issues beyond the compass of teachers' initial training. These developments have, therefore, brought with them the need for further preparation by teachers to introduce, manage and work new policies, changes and innovations. As a form of work, teaching has changed very significantly and so it would be quite appropriate to suggest that teachers, both those in service and those about to embark on a career, need careful preparation in a wide and increasing range of 'basic skills'. Over the last two decades the sophistication of the preparation of beginning teachers has increased significantly in terms of skill development, for example, in terms of assessment techniques, lesson-planning strategies, understandings of learning styles, classroom management, behaviour modification techniques, of progression within subject material, of making provision for pupils with special educational needs, of dealing with pupils from multi-racial backgrounds and many others.

In England and Wales, the formal involvement of serving teachers in the initial training process as mentors can be seen to signify the crucial importance of these aspects, many of which clearly have a very practical nature to them and that, given the rate of introduction of innovations, it is almost only those who are dealing with them literally on a day-to-day basis who stand a chance of being up to date and conversant with practical classroom implications of such developments. Yet there are some drawbacks to this emerging situation.

As with many 'reforms', it is often too easy to achieve an inappropriate balance in trying to rectify past omissions; the pendulum of change can swing too far in opposing directions. In this case, whilst there is little quibble with the clear need for newly trained teachers to be fully conversant with the detailed and often highly skilled techniques needed for effective practice, the 'practical', technical side of their preparation represents only one aspect in what should constitute the preparation of a teacher. The increasing trend whereby the demands of practical preparation have monopolised all of the limited time available in both initial training programmes and in the sphere of in-service preparation, represents an unacceptable hegemony. Exigencies have dictated that such preparation as has been offered to deal with extensive waves of change has been of a short-term, 'quick-fix', 'just-in-time' mode. The elements, therefore, of that which constitutes other parts of the process of teacher preparation will come as little surprise given what has, in earlier sections of this book, been argued for in terms of the need for teachers to be able to reflect, to discuss, to criticise, to think and to locate their practice in creative, imaginative and critical ways within the purposes of schooling. As Lord Judd put it in a debate on the House of Lords in March 1994:

> Teaching is not just a mechanical process by which the curriculum is delivered to pupils. It is absolutely essential that the teacher is reflective and creative; that he or she is master of the subject being taught and preferably with a passion for it. That will become even more essential with the pressures of the century ahead. To encourage thoughtful and creative pupils, demands the same qualities of those

who teach them; and in order to develop those qualities teachers need some theoretical framework within which to consider children's development, addressing their needs and making appropriate judgements about the curriculum. (Hansard 1994)

In the past many teacher initial preparation programmes have been criticised for being 'front loaded'. This has meant that programmes, though much shorter than envisaged in the James Report of 1972, used to begin with a theoretical input from the major contributory disciplines to the field of educational study, philosophy, psychology, sociology and history. Students were often heard to complain that the only time they, as they put it, 'really learned anything' was when they were on teaching practice. In the changed climate at the turn of the century, with both initial and in-service preparation and development, there needs to be a new balance between practical skill development and the theoretical location and critical underpinning of the teachers' role and work. This is illustrated as in Figure 6.1.

Clearly, teachers need significant input in terms of basic skill development early in their preparation, but there should be room here for elements of what has been called 'ecological thinking and reflective capacity' (Bottery and Wright 1996). The model suggested in Figure 6.1 represents a reversal of the approach of the James Report, and of the current practice of front-loading of which the French example referred to earlier is a good example. A similar two-year pattern is found in the German *Länder* where the first phase is broadly theoretical and the second practical (Ofsted 1993).

In England and Wales, the majority of secondary teachers, after completing a degree course, follow a one-year postgraduate programme. The overriding concern of students on such courses is with coping with the

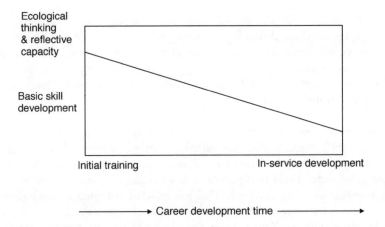

Figure 6.1 Redressing a balance between basic skills and ecological thinking.

demanding aspects of classroom performance. For many teachers, interest in more theoretical, philosophical aspects of teaching develops after they have achieved an element of confidence and security with their classroom practice. There is a logic to substantially reversing present models and that sketched in Figure 6.1 begins to suggest such an approach. As teachers' development progresses during their careers the amount of time devoted to ecological and reflective thinking should be increased commensurate with increased responsibilities in schools, be they managerial, pastoral or curricular. Only by affording teachers time and space to reflect and think will they be able to bring their critical, creative and imaginative capacities to bear on the needs of their learners as together they prepare to live in the uncertain future. The last section in this chapter outlines the role of the teaching profession as an empowering one.

Teaching as an empowering profession

The argument presented in this section culminates in a view of the teaching profession as an empowering profession engaged in the pursuit of an ecologically located debate about its own role and that of the society it exists to serve. Such a view, in aiming to meet the needs of living in uncertainty, is inclusive. Three other possibilities, that of the reprofessionalisation thesis, the failures of both the New Right and the New Modernisers projects and the globalisation/economic determinist debate are examined and rejected in the process of arriving at this point.

It has been argued (Hargreaves 1994) that the conceptions of some who see recent changes to the teaching profession as a 'professionalisation' or re-professionalisation have an inadequate view. This view, he describes as emphasising:

> the struggle for and, in some cases, the realisation of greater teacher professionalism through extensions of the teacher's role. Teachers, especially those in elementary or primary schools, are portrayed as having more experience of whole school curriculum development, involvement in collaborative cultures of mutual support and professional growth. (p. 117)

In commenting on the process of restructuring of teachers' work in the USA, Lawn (1995) suggests that the earlier 'bureaucratisation of schooling made teachers appear as the deliverers of an expert curriculum created elsewhere and sub-divided them into general and specialist teachers, within hierarchies of management' (pp. 349–50). This has now been replaced, through greater devolution, by more control over whole school policy because teachers have new responsibilities. These, he argues, derive from a perception that:

if teaching is the key to new ways of learning, raising standards and levels of pupil achievement, increasing responsiveness to students, new flexible procedures of work, new training emphases and staff development, then teachers will have to be given the freedom to be accountable. (p. 348)

Much of the evidence from the work of Hargreaves (1994) who reports developments from Canada, Woods and Jeffrey (1996) who present findings from four ESRC-funded research projects in England coupled with the empirical evidence presented in earlier chapters of this book has to be considered against such views and more in support of the 'intensification thesis'. This is seen by Hargreaves (1994) as 'a rhetorical ruse, a strategy for getting teachers to collaborate willingly in their own exploitation as more and more effort is extracted from them' (p. 118). The reprofessionalisation thesis, then, does not seem to be supported by these views of the evidence.

The project of the New Right, the introduction of markets into education, has been superseded. To meet the needs of living with uncertainty, where collaboration, communication and collegiality become a strength and asset, the unfettered operation of the market has been increasingly recognised as an unhelpful extension of the Hobbesian 'State of Nature'. The ensuing 'Balkanisation' of schools, their teachers and communities is not appropriate for the likely demands of the future.

The New Modernisers' experiment, where markets are retained but a strong dose of central control (a new Leviathan?) is introduced, is also flawed. For the teacher professional, to work creatively, to be proactive in dealing with uncertainty, there needs to be room for innovation within the system. The trends towards tighter and more exacting restriction in teacher preparation represent an anti-intellectual approach, which is arrogant in its presumption that it possesses the monopoly of right. Without the scope and flexibility for participative regeneration, innovation and dialogues involving all stakeholders in teacher preparation, such monoliths tend in one direction only: atrophy.

Much has been made of arguments deriving from globalisation and economic determinism. David Blunkett, as Secretary of State for Education and Employment in the UK, has advanced this view in his Green Paper *The Learning Age* in the following terms:

Learning is the key to prosperity – for each of us as individuals, as well as for the nation as a whole. Investment in human capital will be the foundation of success in the knowledge-based global economy of the twenty-first century. This is why the Government has put learning at the heart of its ambition. (Blunkett 1998)

The argument against this is not that the pursuit of economic health is intrinsically wrong or a 'bad thing' but that to couch the role of learning and those most closely responsible for promoting it in such an exclusively economic frame will lead to an overall impoverishment both of teachers and, more importantly, the society that they exist to serve.

The argument for an empowering profession is, therefore, first and foremost an inclusive argument. To meet the conditions of uncertainty, present and future citizenry will need flexibility, imagination, creativity, artistry, affective sensibilities as well as cognitive skill and power. So will its teachers. A teaching profession that has been duped into a false professionalism will be unable to decide or recognise where it is being led. Teachers in a New Right mould will be engaged in dog fights in the State of Nature, whilst those of the New Modernisers will be controlled clones, and those solely following the economic rationalist position will find that their future, in human terms, is seriously impoverished. Empowered professionals will be those who seek to enable their clients to maximise their opportunities in the future: opportunities that may be personal, social, spiritual, intellectual, technical, economic, but fundamentally human. It is worth remembering the point made by Reich (1991, p. 1), quoted in Chapter 1:

> All that will remain rooted within national borders are the people who comprise the nation. *Each nation's primary assets will be its citizens' skills and insights*. (Emphasis added.)

The development of these skills and insights will be a central task facing teachers and for which they will need a well-developed capacity for reflective practice and critical thinking, grounded in a research and enquiry-based context. How that is to be developed is the subject of the next chapter.

7

ACTION RESEARCH
AND TEACHER
PROFESSIONALISATION

Introduction

Action research is normally proposed as a means of creating a research culture at the school level, and thereby developing the practice of teachers. It is not normally seen as a means for increasing their impact upon national policy-making. However, because action research is collaborative in nature, because it focuses upon school-led rather than externally driven issues, and because it could provide an extra research dimension to the teaching profession, it is argued here that it could provide a critical underpinning for a heightened teacher status, and therefore for raising the level of impact of the profession upon educational policy-making. This, it is argued, is vital, not only for the good of the profession, but also because a critically aware and reflective teaching profession could become one of the main instruments in a move towards a more just and democratic society. This chapter will critically examine this possibility.

The chapter will briefly set action research within a context of pressures towards deprofessionalisation, before moving to a discussion of different definitions of action research. It will then ask whether it is a sound measure for reasserting a greater degree of professionalism by considering a number of proposed problems with the approach. It will conclude by arguing that it may have to wait for a particular set of facilitatory conditions before it is truly effective, and that an initial best strategy may be one that sees different forms of action research linked in a systematic manner with other professional development.

The pressures for deprofessionalisation

Much recent educational legislation across the Western world parallels a dichotomy within academic literature. Both send mixed messages and conflicting possibilities about personal freedom and political emancipation to practitioners within schools. Thus, on the one hand, writings from a free-market perspective have, as we have seen, acted as a catalyst to legislation, and placed many public-sector professionals in many countries within a scenario where inter-institutional competition for clients is regarded as the norm. In the process, the theory goes, the excesses of bureaucracy are lessened, individual employees, freed from its deadening hand, are encouraged to use their initiative and inventiveness, institutions become more client oriented, and clients themselves become empowered.

There have been undoubted problems with this approach, which have led to the kind of New Modernist modifications described earlier. Thus there have been the damaging effects from competitive practice where co-operation has been more appropriate; there have been gaps in provision because of market-rather than needs-driven imperatives; and there have also been inflated transaction costs through duplication of physical and human resources. All of these have led governments to take a long hard look at the use of markets, and in many cases gradually to place them in a position of subservience to central policy aims. Moreover, the generation of a 'me' culture, and the pursuit of individual wants have led to calls for the need for the return of a greater degree of trust and a greater sense of community. Having said this, market-generated policies still have their influence; the promise of individual empowerment and fulfilment through flatter organisational structures, greater individual responsibility and initiative remains an attractive one to public and policy-makers alike.

Yet as we have argued, such a philosophy has never actually dominated policy agendas. It has almost always been accompanied by one geared to a different set of managerialist imperatives, described by Hood (1991) as the 'New Public Management'. This second perspective is more concerned with professional control, with the most 'rational' generation of economies and efficiencies within an uncritically accepted policy framework. It is well illustrated by the meaning of Total Quality Management given by Murgatroyd and Morgan (1993, p. 121).

> Basic empowerment begins when the vision and goals have already been set by the school leaders. What a team or an individual is empowered to do is to turn the vision and strategy into reality through achieving those challenging goals set for them by the leadership of the school. *Individuals are being empowered in terms of how they can achieve the goals set, not in terms of what the goals might be.* (Our italics.)

Here is a very different message from that of the market, one that suggests that responsibility, fulfilment, empowerment, and initiative are to be circumscribed and directed by organisational and external policy imperatives. Thus Smyth (1993) argues that much of the move towards local financial management, in the UK and in much of the rest of the Western world, rather than primarily being a free-market move to energise individual inventiveness and

126

responsiveness, is in reality designed to devolve responsibility – and the problems that go with this – down to 'units' (schools, hospitals etc.), whilst the centre retains control over policy and purposes. Indeed, whilst it is possible to interpret the influential writings of Caldwell and Spinks on the 'self-managing school' within a free-market framework in their original publication in 1988, this is clearly not the case a decade later (Caldwell and Spinks 1998). By this time their espousal of the role of schools as implementers of centralist legislation in inventive but policy-devoid ways is strikingly clear. Their message for the functioning of schools in much of the Western world is one of uncritical implementation.

Similarly, and somewhat paradoxically considering his position in a centralising Labour government in education in England and Wales, M. Barber (1995, p. 52) pointed out that the teaching profession is being managerially dismembered, that the profession is being 'carved up among a variety of government agencies'. He described this in detail:

> The School Curriculum and Assessment Authority establishes what teachers should teach; the Teacher Training Agency decides how they should be trained to teach it; the Office for Standards in Education decides whether they are teaching it well; and the School Teachers' Review Body decides how much they should be paid for their efforts.

Nothing has changed since he wrote this, save some of the quangos' names, particularly when he argues: 'Lurking behind these agencies is the Government's Department for Education which appoints their members and sets out their responsibilities.'

This 'post-Fordist' analysis of societies[1] thus locates the teacher at the bottom of an implementation pyramid, with those in senior management teams ceasing to have an important hand in policy direction. On this scenario, the most they can expect is an entrepreneurial 'buzz' from devising new ways of 'selling' their institution to potential 'consumers'. This is then only control of the determination of the how to implement directives, not the what. The picture for those at the bottom is even more bleak. They are twice removed from real empowerment, real initiative. The first level of disempowerment is that of government. In the UK, this is the Department for Education and Employment and its various agencies like the QCA, Ofsted, and the TTA controlling policy. The second level is provided by the Senior Management Teams (SMTs) of schools, who dictate implementation. The average class teacher is then left with little more than the implementing, in the process creating much of the current picture of low teacher morale and high stress levels. It is also one important strand within the construction of a progressive teacher deprofessionalisation.[2]

Now, of course there are usually ways of modifying or subverting legislative requirements. We are still some considerable way from Foucault's image of the

Panopticon accomplishing a complete and self-administered surveillance of workers within the workplace (Sewell and Wilkinson 1992). Class teachers can still take many individual decisions about the style and content of teaching and learning in the classroom. Further, whilst more thoughtful SMTs are worried by teacher disempowerment (not least because this is a reflection of their own policy disempowerment), even the less concerned require class teacher collaboration to be effective. Nevertheless, this is a recipe for teacher deprofessionalisation. If the three most regularly cited criteria for professionalism[3] are expertise, autonomy, and altruism, then, by placing the average teacher on the lowest rung of a policy ladder, many post-Fordist moves critically erode the first two, and cast seriously into doubt their ability to maintain allegiance to the third.

Whilst it is undoubtedly the case that some professional aspirations are more self- than other-serving, and that therefore the demise of professional power needs only to be of concern to teachers themselves, this book has argued that a properly conceptualised version of professionalism is essential to the lifeblood of a democracy. If, as argued elsewhere (Bottery 1998), such a concept contains within it an appreciation of the need to educate the client in the dilemmas of decision-making, in the subjectivity of judgement, and in the need and increasing ability of such clients to participate in decision-making, professionals could be instrumental in developing an empowered and informed citizenry who were educated by such professionals in the impact of legislation on their practice, and on the likely outcome of such legislation and societal change upon citizens' lives. Such professionals would thereby broaden and flatten decision-making in society, and contribute in a significant and meaningful way to the development of a genuinely participatory democracy.

The teaching profession then has a crucial role to play, not only in the more obvious task in the development of learning, but also in the development of citizenship. Indeed, it should be argued that a proper conceptualisation of the former must incorporate an adequate conception of the latter – and lead to its development. However, if the teaching profession were to be so emasculated that it contributed little to policy formation, and did little more than implement the policies of others, then they would be seriously limited in any attempt to develop either. The research of this book suggests that such times may already be with us, in that virtually all the in-service education and training investigated appeared to be devoted to questions of legislative implementation. It has prompted the question of whether teachers were collaborating in their own deprofessionalisation, for if one is seriously committed to the belief that a profession limited to a technical-rationalist orientation has grave consequences for both its own development and that of the society within which it is situated, then there appears to be an urgent need for the teaching profession (and not just its leaders) to take steps to reassert its interest and responsibility in matters beyond the classroom.

Locating action research within a climate of deprofessionalisation

So what opportunities are there for reasserting teacher professionalism and the importance of teachers' opinions in matters of policy? A first step is for the teaching profession to take the issue of deprofessionalisation seriously, and to devote time to enlarging the profession's understanding of the implications of legislative and societal change upon its role in society. M. Barber (1995) argued that too much legislation is devoted to the 'known universe' of education – to the determination of structure and policies – and too little to the 'unknown' – the relation between pupil and teacher. He suggests that one cannot legislate quality into existence from above, but that changes must be made at the level of practice. Significantly, since he wrote this, the new Labour government in the United Kingdom has changed its focus to the 'unknown', but has done so by intervening, advising and legislating on 'best practice'. In the process, the 'unknown' has become the 'known' of yet more centralist direction. Indeed, as Tomlinson (1995, p. 65) argued in the same volume as Barber: '... our greatest danger is the discarding of the personal responsibility of the individual teacher through an excess of external direction, control and measurement ...'.

There seems to be agreement that the school and the teacher must be the focal points for change. Yet if such changes are to occur at this level, this book would argue that they must be understood, developed and owned by those whose culture is to change. They must certainly stem primarily from work within schools. Nevertheless, they must address issues beyond the school that impinge upon such practice. There are a number of ways in which this consciousness-raising exercise could be performed.

Schools could, for instance, set aside specific periods of in-service education to debate such issues. This need not be done separately, but as a specified part of a curriculum or management issue. It would then bring home the point of Barr and McGhie (1995) that perhaps we should think carefully about the usefulness of a term like 'values education', with its suggestion that this is the province of 'moral education' or 'values education' specialists. Instead, it is crucial that all teachers appreciate that they should be concerned about values in education, for values inter-penetrate all aspects of school life.

Schools could also utilise an increasingly important strategy developed in business, and an integral part of the development of student teachers – that of mentoring (e.g. Wilkin 1992; McIntyre, Hagger and Wilkin 1993). Whilst this has potential for an influential 'other' to help develop the potentialities of younger teachers, it has the serious limitation of presently being insufficiently conceptualised for a 'critical' role. More importantly, it is essentially concerned with one-to-one relationships, whereas a genuine attempt to foster the professionalisation of the teaching profession must aim to develop team links between them.

Schools may then be better utilising a particular collaborative approach, extensively recommended as a means to teacher emancipation, that of action research. Whilst action research has undergone a number of changes in its scope, methodology, and purpose, it has been seen as a prime means of restoring the authority of teachers by raising their professional status through making their practice the central location for research (e.g. Stenhouse 1975, Elliott 1993, Carr and Kemmis 1986). It is also, and significantly, seen by the TTA in the UK as a primary means of upgrading teachers' skills in the delivery of various aspects of national policy. So what precisely is it? It is necessary to consider definitions.

Definitions

There have been a number of definitions of action research over the years. In their extensive bibliographical review, Hult and Lennung (1980) point to an action research tradition in schools, in the community, and in organisational studies. Moreover it is possible to perceive an historical development from an early action research paradigm,[4] of small groups fine-tuning the application of researchers' theories and findings to their specific situations, through to one that believed that the research itself should be located and developed at the practitioner level. Nevertheless, it still seems possible to identify five essential features of the approach. Thus, firstly, action research is more concerned with improving the practice of those within an immediate situation than it is with developing any theoretical overview, or developing principles that might be applied to other situations.

Secondly, it is eclectic in the adoption of relevant procedures. Whilst Hodgkinson (1957) could bemoan teachers' lack of sophistication in statistical procedures, much less emphasis would now be placed on a particular research strategy or evaluative procedure. Increasingly, action research is seen as catholic in its acceptance of the appropriateness of techniques, these being determined by the problem and the context within which that problem is found (see, for instance, Altrichter, Posch and Somekh 1993).

Thirdly, it believes that practice improvement is brought about by a concentration upon process rather than product, upon formative rather than summative evaluation. Further, one should expect a spiral process involving problem specification, review, diagnosis, planning, implementation, and the monitoring of effects, after which other issues will probably become relevant and demand attention.

Fourthly, action research is underpinned by a belief in the need for collaboration. It therefore has increasingly tended to eschew the separation of researcher and subject, instead believing that better research is a result of where all those involved contributed their understanding. As Hodgkinson (1957, p. 139) said:

Action research is a direct and logical outcome of the progressive position. After showing children how to work together to solve their problems, the next step was for teachers to adopt the methods they had been teaching their children, and learn to solve their own problems co-operatively.

Finally, and following from this, it is essentially bottom-up in orientation. Thus, if it is committed to solving the problems of those within a particular context, and if it believes that these problems are best identified and defined by those within this context, then it follows that it must begin with their orientation and their understanding, rather than with any definition produced from above.

The promise and problems of action research

Now, in theory at least, action research would appear to present teachers with an excellent opportunity for the reassertion of professionalism. Thus:

- by shifting the focus of research to the examination and solution of school-based problems, it should improve their practice, and hence raise their status;
- by locating the focus of research within schools, it could raise the profile of the teaching profession with the general public, and could provide them with extended opportunities to acquaint the public with the issues with which they have to deal;
- it would extend their expertise, and therefore their professional identity; teachers could become in the eyes of the public as much researchers as implementers, with all the increased status that accrues to researchers;
- it should, by making them more reflective and research-oriented practitioners, also render them more effective in their practice;
- the research dimension of teaching could provide a focus for a more collaborative – and therefore more effective and influential – profession.

Questions of adoption

Nevertheless, before these promises could be recognised as probabilities one must ask whether action research is capable of fulfilling this role. The problems are to be seen at six different levels: the theoretical, the philosophical, the personal, the classroom, the institutional, and the societal levels.

Theoretical level

Questions of a practical nature will probably have a more immediate effect upon the chances of action research being adopted as a measure to upgrade teacher professionalism. Nevertheless, its appeal would be seriously undermined should it be seen as theoretically implausible. Such questions must be dealt with initially.

Now, whilst there are problems with action research as a species of qualitative method,[5] there are more pressing criticisms of action research in its own right. The criticisms of a particular branch – critical action research – will be left until later. Here, two difficulties generic to this approach will be dealt with. They are:

- that it fails to qualify as research proper because it is not disinterested;
- that some proponents of action research appear to suggest that it can (even, must) dispense with the need for theory.

Lack of disinterest

This criticism was put pithily by Johnson (1994), when she wrote (p. 35):

> Action research has the aim of bringing immediate improvement to an ongoing programme, rather than making an assessment of a situation as it stands (as other forms of research tend to do), then providing recommendations for future change. My problem is that interventionist tinkering of this kind does not equate with my view of research.

It is clear from the 'interventionist tinkering' jibe that Johnson believes that action research does not even qualify as research. Research is seen as 'making an assessment of the situation' (in contrast to 'bringing immediate improvements to an ongoing programme'). However, research is seen as providing 'recommendations for change'. But so, it might be argued, is the action research programme. The difference appears to be in that many recommendations in action research occur during formative assessment, rather than the summative assessment of Johnson's preferred research. However, it is not clear why formative assessment (if its insights are sensibly incorporated into an ongoing programme) should not contribute to the improvement of a situation just as much as summative forms. Research is then seen on both accounts as being of use to a practice situation – and so neither are disinterested. Both, to different degrees, show commitment, and commitment is only a problem where it prevents participants from being open-minded about the data gained and the theories of practice produced. This is more a matter of individual integrity than methodology, and does not seem to invalidate action research.

Eschewal of theory

A second question is the implication in some action research literature that it can dispense with theory, because it is in essence an activity designed to improve teachers' practice, not to add to some particular body of scientific literature. As Beattie (1989, p. 111) says:

> It is a primary tenet of action research that practice should be informed by, and be a test of, some idea generated by reflection on what one has observed in the classroom. As the action is carried out, one observes the effects that it has and then reflects upon their significance for the initial hypothesis. In the light of one's results, one devises a new, related action. Thus practice and theory are seen as moments in the process of devising, carrying out, and reflecting upon, intentional actions.

Were it to follow from this that the only relevant – and therefore valid – research is that carried out by practitioners, such an orientation would probably relegate action research to the level and theory of common-sense and classroom reflection. Yet, as Beattie (1989, p. 114) points out, there are a number of levels of theory (substantive grounded theories, grounded formal theories, grand theories) which may all be useful to educationalists, and which improve their practice by placing their own reflection within some kind of perspective. There are also meta-theories which underpin practice and provide a means for understanding and rationally assessing it. Thus, John Elliott (1993)uses the work of Gadamer to underpin his account of action research, whilst Carr and Kemmis (1986) use that of Habermas. And yet, were action research theorists to refuse to accept the place of theory and meta-theory, they would be in danger of cutting the intellectual ground out from underneath themselves. They would also be in danger, as Beattie (1989, p. 18) points out, of committing precisely the sin of which they accuse others:

> The suspicion arises that an attempt is being made to steer the practice of action research. Yet is this not to violate its basic commitment to practitioner control over research questions, purposes and methods?

The danger here for action research is the 'baby with the bath water' syndrome: that whilst there is genuine virtue in raising the status of teacher theory and perspectives, there is little virtue in stipulating that this is the only valid perspective or level of theory. Indeed, if, as most action researchers believe, there are real benefits to be gained from the kind of reflective practice opened up by the work of John Dewey (1933), and, more recently, by Argyris and Schön (1974) and Schön (1983), then they must accept that an essential aspect of good practice is precisely the opening up to others' perspectives on the problem. In particular, this means moving from what Argyris and Schön describe as a 'Level 1' theory, which works by changing or improving procedures and behaviours within accepted paradigms, to a 'Level 2' theory, which questions the assumptions upon which the paradigm is built, and therefore has a more profound effect upon beliefs as well as behaviours. Such 'Level 2' theorising is possible only by the willing utilisation of others' understandings and theories. The bottom line appears to be this: if teachers' perspectives have been neglected in research in the past, they (and action research proponents) do themselves no favours by neglecting the perspectives of those who have neglected them. Whilst the focus needs to be at the level of professional practice, such practice can only be enriched by an appreciation of the best research and perspectives – from wherever that may derive.

Problems of critical action research

If action research is to act as a vehicle for improved teacher status, then it must ask the right questions. Critical action research, it is claimed, raises issues necessary for developing teacher consciousness which other forms neglect. Perhaps the most celebrated example of such an approach in educational action research is Carr and Kemmis's (1986) *Becoming Critical*. In this book, they argue against two other models, suggesting that both of these are inadequate as models for participatory action research. The first, the positivist model, based as it is upon a belief in the applicability of the procedures originally used in the study of the physical sciences, suggests that it is possible to construct a value-free educational science. Following Habermas (1972) and Kuhn (1970), however, Carr and Kemmis argue that observations cannot be neutral, that they are dependent for their selection, description and evaluation in the light of the particular theory within which the scientist works. Furthermore, because participants and observers may have different agendas, the intention of a behaviour may be interpreted by an observer in a totally different way from that of the actor. In support of this, they quote (p. 88) Ayer, who suggests that raising and drinking a glass of wine can be interpreted as 'an act of self-indulgence, an expression of politeness, a manifestation of loyalty, a gesture of despair, an attempt at suicide, a religious communication . . .'. In other words, observations cannot be theory- or value-neutral, and if this is the case, then by failing to acknowledge and question this theory-dependence, they implicitly support the value status quo, whatever that is.

The second model, the interpretive model, acknowledges the value standpoints of observers and participants, and takes as its *raison d'être* the explication of the understanding of actors of the situation within which they participate. Nevertheless, this is also seen as ultimately unsatisfactory because, it is claimed, such description fails to acknowledge that such intentions and acts exist within particular power structures, and that such power structures distort people's perception of what ought to be the case.

By neglecting this aspect, interpretative models, it is suggested, are inherently conservative, for they merely describe and reflect existing societal conditions and beliefs. A critical theory, on the other hand, provides individuals with an understanding of such power structures, and of how such structures – and the ideologies behind them – can distort understanding of what is the case, of what are their real interests. If the aim of a positivist model is to describe a reality, and that of an interpretive model is to describe the different perceptions of that reality, the critical model's aim is to enlighten, and to emancipate groups by helping them to recognise their true interests. It will be clear that a critical theory perspective, pointing up as it does power structures and actors' interests, might have considerable relevance to a profession seeking to pursue a larger role in educational policy-making. Nevertheless, if critical theorists point out the inadequacies of other meta-theories, they are not without problems themselves. Two will be mentioned here.

Firstly, critical theory, derived as it is essentially from a Marxist perspective, is usually underpinned by some form of teleological belief – that history is moving inexorably towards some ideal future state. This, it would seem, is intellectual baggage for critical theory which is difficult to sustain. Indeed, an emancipatory critical theory has no logical necessity for such teleological underpinning, and it would certainly be credible to develop a critical theory that held to a belief in power structures and oppression, and an ethic of emancipation from them, without necessarily subscribing to the belief that this was, or needed to be, an illustration of some single grand design. A picture without the historicism of a teleological golden sunset may more accurately depict things as they are, as well as providing critical theory with a more secure base.

Secondly, and similarly, some critical theory takes the line of a single and unitary source of oppression, with the attendant suggestion that one must be either for or against emancipation in some holistic sense. More plausible is Hammersley's (1992, p. 111) suggestion, which is that structures of oppression are multiple in origin, and differentially effective, depending upon time, place, oppressor and oppressee. Such a move would obviate charges of simplicity, whilst not affecting the viability of an emancipatory intention – though it would force emancipators to look very carefully at the context of each emancipation!

Philosophical level

There is, however, a deeper problem with emancipation which reflects a current and major debate in philosophy. If the primary aim of critical action research is emancipation, then its major criterion of validity must be the effectiveness of this emancipation. Yet this has a number of problems. For instance, who is to judge this effectiveness? Is it the emancipated? But who is to say that their understanding is still not ideologically distorted? And what if some feel emancipated, and others do not? Which do we use then? Carr and Kemmis's (1986, Ch. 5) appeal to Habermas's 'ideal speech situations' as a way out of this problem was, as even they admitted, extremely tentative. Indeed, since then, Carr has gone on to suggest (1995) that Habermas belongs to the same category of 'modernist' writers as R. S. Peters; thinkers who falsely pursued a universal rationalism which could rise above situation and circumstance. Carr (p. 87) now argues along post-modernist lines that:

> ... there is nothing external to experience, no essence to human nature, no human destiny towards which history moves. Instead, there are just human beings shaping and being shaped by their history as they make their way through an uncertain world shot through with contingency – a world that is always incomplete and always in the making.

This has huge implications for education in general, and action research in particular. Much of the driving force for education over the last two hundred years has been based upon Enlightenment notions of human progress which utilises a universal reason to suggest the possibility of transcending the rules and values of particular societies, to point to something more timelessly and universally human. Without this intellectual framework, the very possibility of a meaningful philosophy of education is called seriously into question, for education, post-modernist thought suggests, like all other branches of human thought, is so ineradicably imprisoned within the frames that shape our consciousnesses, that it can only provide a justification for the values and beliefs of the social order of its time.

If this is true, then critical action research, wedded to the idea of emancipation, must face the same kinds of question. What can emancipation mean if a person is merely 'a centreless configuration mediated and constituted through the discourses learned and acquired in becoming a participant in a historical culture' (Carr, 1995, p. 80), who therefore has no access to extra-contextual meaning or analysis? Such post-modernist pessimism would be extremely corrosive to any project that wishes to use any notion of human progress to underpin a critique of existing conditions.

In his paper, Carr attempts a tricky balancing act between the objectivity of universalism, and the relativism of post-modern determinism. Rather like his namesake, the historian E. H. Carr (1982), he suggests that despite a subjectivism of perception and value, individuals can nevertheless use their awareness of their groundedness to compare it with that of others – and thus to provide a different lens upon their 'reality', and perhaps through that to provide some criteria for acceptable progress and emancipation.

This brief description of an extremely dense area, can do little more than suggest that, at the philosophic level, emancipatory action research has questions to answer. Whether such questions actually impinge upon the level of policy, is probably just as problematic. Nevertheless, a system that fails at this level will, sooner or later, find such criticisms filtering up to the practical.

Personal level

However, even if theoretically and philosophically acceptable, action research must also be practically viable, or it will not get off the ground. At a personal level, many teachers will question whether a more critical professionalism is high on their list of priorities, and, even more so, whether their role as teacher encompasses political emancipation. They may accept that a teaching profession needs a larger voice in policy-making, and that there are things wrong with society but, through a combination of implementation pressures, and in the case of emancipation, a lack of conviction in the degree to which they or others are oppressed, may simply fail to respond to such arguments.

Critical action research has to be careful here. If it is truly committed to the emancipation of teachers through these same teachers choosing research projects, then it must in principle permit them to choose projects of a technical rationalist or interpretive nature. If critical theorists then attempt to impose their emancipatory theories upon an unimpressed teaching profession, they may be accused of simply substituting their own authoritarianism for that of another. To be fair, Carr and Kemmis acknowledge (1986, p. 201) that:

> Those who intervene in the life of groups concerned with education
> to establish communities of action researchers are frequently regarded
> as 'manipulators' who are in fact responsible for the action taken by
> these groups.

Moreover, they are careful not to exclude examples of action research that are not of a critical orientation. However, they do not seem satisfactorily to resolve the problem of external influence. Teachers who (in critical eyes) are labouring under a false consciousness, are unlikely to adopt the projects and critical strategies that would bring about their emancipation until they are critically aware, which they cannot be precisely because of this lack of the appropriate projects and strategies.

This problem does not apply as much to a critique that is more directly interested in teachers' professional development than in more overt forms of political emancipation, even though, in the long run, the two may aim at much the same thing. However, teachers, oppressed in terms of overwork and lack of time, and working within a culture that does not reward those critical of external policy, may well restrict the focus of their action research projects to the immediately heuristic. The only way this would change is if they were given the encouragement and the time to engage in something more personally expansive – and this is an issue beyond the personal.

Classroom level

It seems clear from the literature that whilst there are examples of exclusively school-generated action research projects, most documented projects have been contributory studies to an individual teacher's higher degree qualification, and that these projects have tended to run out of steam when this incentive has been taken away. In other words, action research has generally failed to become part of the culture of most schools. This may be down to the inability of teachers to appreciate its benefits. More likely is that if teachers are busy implementing governmental directives, wading through national attainment tests, working out how to meet specified targets, or are preparing for external inspections, initiatives like action research may be seen, in an age of personal and institutional survival, as luxuries for a distant, less stressful future. The issue then becomes a political one of getting the concept of action research onto school agendas, and making its use part of the cultural fabric of the school. Initial moves by the Teacher Training Agency in the late 1990s in the UK to generate such enthusiasm, as a way of improving curricular implementation, and therefore of developing a (restricted) professionalism, have so far had limited impact.

Such encouragement is helpful, but pragmatically it is most likely to be taken up if it is enthusiastically adopted and facilitated by a school's senior management team. Without this, it is unlikely to happen. Yet there seems good reason to believe that this may not happen, and this is because both teachers and senior management teams may believe that the teacher has a basically different mission in the classroom from that of the researcher. Wong (1995, p. 23) puts it bluntly when he suggests that 'the primary goal of research is to understand; the primary goal of teaching is to help students learn'.

Wong gives the personal example of taking a full class discussion and encountering within it a student who was experiencing difficulties with one of his questions. His research orientation suggested that he spend time analysing why this student was having such problems; yet his teaching commitment told him that such delay would do little for the student's understanding or confidence. Moreover, by pursuing such a research-oriented strategy, he felt he was in grave danger of undermining the flow of the class discussion. As he says (p. 28): 'although my role as researcher was optional, my role as teacher was not. At all times I had a moral and legal responsibility to treat students with compassion and create experiences that were educationally valuable.' Wong suggests that reconciliation is possible;

but only by changing the classroom culture to one where the students are educated to understand the research element of the teaching process and, further, are encouraged to be equal participants in the process. This is no easy option, meaning, as it does, not just a change to classroom routines but challenges to the fundamental assumptions of many who work within schools.

Institutional level

A central tenet of action research is its collaborative nature; a central tenet of critical action research is its necessarily critical democratic spirit. The two are not necessarily the same. The latter is more subversive of the status quo than the former, in encouraging the questioning of given authority and imposed rules. Now whilst Carr and Kemmis (1986) caution against a too radical choice of project by the researcher, there is little doubt that such projects will challenge – and are designed to challenge – the existing power structures of many schools. A necessary question, then, is: What will – or can – Senior Management Teams allow? In an age of managed schools, where many measures of success are dictated by external bodies, Senior Management Teams may out of conviction, but many more out of habit, believe that any action research that takes place will come into being only if it fits the management plan for the school as a whole. This seems to be as nice a case of Hargreaves' (1994) 'contrived collegiality' if ever there was one. Individual teachers selecting their own research foci will then probably be seen in many schools as at best non-contributory to such plans, at worst, working against them. In such a climate, emancipatory action research will be very difficult to engender.

What of the more limited notion of action research as a vehicle for the development of the profession, the kind that one assumes the UK Teacher Training Agency espouses? Whilst not as threatening as 'political' critical action research, it still faces considerable problems. The research presented in this book suggests that much 'professional development' consists of little more than a diet of short courses on implementation issues. Issues of the 'public' or 'ecological' kind raised in this book hardly get a look in. However, this is probably not due to any ideological commitment against such provision – as it may be with that of an emancipatory kind – but rather due more to an issue raised again and again; that of time and pressure. The situation here, then, is pessimistic, but not terminal.

Societal level

Two influences will be raised in this section, one long term, one medium term, which seem to run counter to the development of action research as a means of raising teacher professionalism.

The first suggests that an analysis of professionalism needs to be located within a wider post-Fordist analysis of society, in which policy is retained at the centre, whilst responsibility for implementation is moved out to the periphery – the school. On such an analysis, then, the intensification of external standards and inspection, of managerialism, and of contrived collegiality, are all symptomatic of the same strategy, seen not only in education, the health sector, and other public institutions, but within the business community as well (Bottery 1994, 1998). If this is the case, then a major – possibly the major – constraint, is going to be the very fabric within which society's institutions cloak themselves, which then tends to frame and direct the consciousness and values of its inhabitants. Action research, which seeks to locate some degree of policy determination at the periphery, may well be running against the trend. Evidence for such a view is to be found in research by Lauriala and Syrjala (1995), who describe the implementation of teacher-centred action research strategies in Finland as becoming viable only after a move away from the kinds of centralised prescriptivity currently to be seen in many countries with respect to teacher education, and towards a more varied and school-based approach, and an increased interest in alternative pedagogies, including action research. In countries where there are moves to centralise teacher education, this will militate against any moves towards a heightened teacher professionalisation, and any increased input on policy.

The second influence runs to the very heart of the adoption of 'bottom-up' packages. As Olson (1989) points out, Schön (1983) offers an interesting analysis of why reflective practice is difficult to accomplish, yet he says much less about the persistence of technical rationality – the persistence by professionals of failing to use their own judgement, and instead adopting techniques, patterns of behaviour, and practice packages designed elsewhere. Olson concludes that the reason has much to do with the need for security, to avoid blame, to make action 'less hazardous':

'Look' says the educator 'I acted on the basis of the best science available. You cannot blame me if things did not come out well: blame the science-based procedures that guided me . . .' The appeal to science allows the professional to off-set the risks of action by evoking the mandate and the mantle of science – of technical rationality. (p. 104)

What is doubly disturbing is that trends may be exacerbating this situation, rather than reducing it. Thus, if professionals feel that they are being scrutinised more and more, that their practice is becoming more accountable, and that society is becoming increasingly litigious (Dingwall 1994), it is not surprising if teachers, for instance, develop a love–hate relationship with detailed centralised prescriptivity. It might constrain their professional practice, and lead them down pedagogic roads they might feel inappropriate, but it is a useful scapegoat to blame if results do not come out as they or others might want them. Even the use of competition as the principal form of centralised policy imposition will not help this situation, for the evidence seems to suggest that a competitive market in education may instead create institutions that are afraid to try new things and fail. Thus research in the United States, both in education (Moore 1990), and in the health care sector (Culyer and Posnett 1990) suggests that this is the case, that competition does not necessarily provide variety. Rather it tends to promote a conservatism of provision. If this continues to be borne out, then action research projects, which run counter to a technical rationalist orientation, and encourage trial and error, will be running against societal trends.

Action research in a more facilitative context

This chapter has examined a number of definitions of action research, and looked at some of the problems involved in it being used as a vehicle for raising teachers' professional status. It seems fair to conclude that some forms of in-service education and professional development (and within this would be included types of action research) may be hard pressed to make an impact upon many educational agendas. These would seem to include:

- those that are seen as overtly political and/or teleological in nature;
- those seen as exacerbating present teaching concerns of time, implementation, and stress;
- those that appear to conflict with the ethical responsibilities to students arising from the requirements of teaching;
- those that leave teachers feeling insecure and exposed to criticism.

It might be felt, given such a hefty list, that action research is currently a very small stone in the sling of a professional David setting out to fight an overwhelmingly powerful post-Fordist, political Goliath. The only difference now is that this time David has no hope of winning. There must be a degree of truth in this. Action research is not likely to have much effect, by itself, upon dominant trends within many current political and economic cultures. If one divides forms of action research into the technical rationalist, the interpretive, and the critical, then the technical rationalist, single-loop approach, seems the one most consonant with present pressures and is the orientation most likely to be adopted. This is because it seems to be the one most easily incorporated within top-down specifications of what a teaching staff should be devoting their research to, largely because it fails to question paradigms in use. It is certainly the only kind being encouraged by bodies like the Teacher Training Agency in England and Wales.

However, even within the current climate, the prospect is not that gloomy, for the forms of action research are not rigidly separate, but merge into one another. Thus, calls by the TTA for a 'research and evidence-based profession' are very clearly calls for a profession to develop research and evidence to show what is the best way of implementing TTA agendas. Yet technical rationalist calls like these give rise to 'interpretive' agendas fairly quickly. After all, good teaching demands an awareness of others' understandings and needs and any research that begins to view issues from a number of angles, particularly within education, invariably begins to point to issues of a critical nature. Given the right conditions, one might have good reason for believing it could transmute into something far more active and conducive to teacher professionalism. For example, the kind of research being engendered within the Birmingham Local Education Authority for headteachers, based largely around the qualitative work of Peter Ribbins (Ribbins and Marland 1994), could provide the kind of SMT impetus that might undergird a wider teacher professionalisation.

Nevertheless, for action research to have an appreciable impact, it must be located within a framework that facilitates this effect. Such a framework would need at least three facilitating conditions:

1   It would require governments committed to the idea that teaching quality is raised at least as much by improving the quality of teachers as by increasing accountability procedures. Such a commitment would be shown, partly by a declared trust in the ability of teachers to develop their own agendas for research, but also, and crucially, by the provision of time and money for teachers to develop such locally based research. There is little sign that this is happening with the many governments that adopt a 'low trust/high accountability' attitude to teachers at present. On the other hand, given that there is a strong business literature suggesting that trust is a valuable management tool, and that high accountability strategies appear to be driving down the numbers of people wanting to enter such a crucial profession for social stability and regeneration, there may still be room for optimism here.

2   Such a facilitating framework would require that teacher education, from initial teacher training onwards, gave time and consideration to the long-term future of the teaching profession, and of its contribution to education policy. The kind of 'normative' action research advocated by Baburoglu and Ravn (1992), which stresses the need for stakeholders to articulate and aim to achieve preferred states of the world, rather than merely aiming to address current short-term problems, would fit well with such a requirement. M. Barber's (1995) proposals further highlight this as an urgent area for consideration.

3   Finally, and perhaps most importantly, teachers have to accept the responsibility and the aspiration of being members of a profession that does more than provide innovative implementations of legislation, but also sees itself as advancing the frontiers of educational knowledge. It has

to have not only a respect for research, but a genuine desire to engage in it. Action research could be its primary tool. However, teachers have to want to aspire to this conception of a profession; responsibility can be given, but it has to be taken as well.

Given such conditions, there are other strategies for remediation which could link in with action research to produce a synergistic effect. Mentoring and appraisal, for instance, could both contribute to the development of a wider appreciation of the professional role of the teacher. If, at the present time, the former seems devoted predominantly to the technical development of student teachers, whilst the latter seems to be increasingly utilised as a tool for the development of senior management strategies, there is no reason to believe they could not have a much greater emancipatory effect within the kind of facilitatory framework described above.

All of this points yet again to the reappraisal of in-service provision in schools. Schools should set aside specific time for consideration and deliberation of issues beyond those of curricular and managerial implementation. In-service education should focus attention upon the 'public' dimension of teaching, as well as spending more time upon the 'ecological' dimension of schooling – locating the practice of teaching within wider political and social issues, thereby deepening the teaching profession's understanding of these – and of itself. These dimensions lead to two further appreciations:

- A first remediative awareness is that teaching is suffused with values at all levels of its theory and practice. Teachers appreciate that 'values education' is not be the province of a specialist; values are in all education. The teaching profession's duty to grapple with them is a *sine qua non* of good education.
- Alongside such an awareness must come a further appreciation of the need to move from single-loop to double-loop learning. The ability to criticise not only practices but the paradigms within which such practices are located must be seen as a necessary requirement for all professionals worthy of the name.

Taken together, and within a facilitatory framework, such approaches could have a major effect upon the culture and expectations of the teaching profession.

Conclusion

If current post-Fordist and managerialist constraints continue to operate on action, then action research, as other critical approaches, will have a hard time of it over the next few years, operating as they do in many ways counter to such culture. Action research in particular will remain a small stone in the teaching profession's sling. However, within a more facilitatory framework, it could have a major effect upon the development of a reconstructed teaching profession. It would need to be seen, however, as locating its practices within theoretical traditions that have consciously articulated value bases, as consisting of different levels of critical strength, and, finally, as being one strategy amongst others in the development of a greater teacher professionalisation. Action research on its own, then, will not deliver the pot of gold at the end of the professional rainbow. However, given the right conditions, it could be one of its primary colours.

8

CONCLUSION

Introduction

This book has so far produced both argument and research to suggest that many governmental policies, as well as the attitudes of many in the teaching profession, are focused on the predictable, the measurable, and the here-and-now. The approach by government may give some in power comfort in the spurious belief that greater control and direction of a teaching profession will facilitate more focused and strategising policy-making in the future, just as the focus of the teaching profession upon curricular and pastoral issues may give such teachers comfort in the belief that they are attending to the pressing concerns of students. But, ultimately, the first must fail because increased control only exacerbates a problem of adaptation in an age of increasing change, and the second must fail because it fails to address the context within which such curricular and pastoral issues occur. This final chapter will then address the question of change at individual, communal and global levels, whilst asking what kind of a teaching profession is required for the new millennium.

Change, the individual human, and the individual ant

Much economic literature is predicated on the idea of the rational, self-interested individual making choices based upon a cost-benefit analysis of the range of possible alternatives. This kind of thinking not only dominates much economic thinking, it has infected much political and social thinking over the last two decades as well. Yet this is a false picture of humanity, and a misleading view of the manner in which individuals approach the question of change. Human beings do not make choices in this simplistic, additive manner. If they did, it would be relatively easy to predict how people would choose, and therefore relatively easy to factor this into any predictions of large-scale change.

Yet individual human choice is not as simple as that. Indeed, individual ant behaviour is much more complex than that. In his book *Butterfly Economics*

(1998), Paul Ormerod describes a series of experiments with an ant colony concerning their behaviour with regard to two identical food sources. These food sources were at the same distances from the colony, and were constantly replenished in order that they remained identical. There was then no reason for one food source to be preferred to another. Given this situation, the question was: how would the ants divide themselves up with respect to this food?

A first thought might be that they would divide equally. A little more thought might lead one to believe that, as with the toss of a coin, any number of variations is possible, though over time one would expect that these proportions would come near to a 50:50 split. However, here a complication is added. It is a known fact that when ants are returning with food, they stimulate other ants leaving the nest to follow their trail by chemical secretion. So now the situation is one where ants will influence others, and where these other ants will always find food, because the experimenters have always kept the food supply topped up.

It should be clear that the random decisions by the first ants leaving the nest will exert a disproportionate effect upon the number of subsequent ants visiting one site or another. If the first half-dozen ants, for example, all go the northern pile, and induce those coming out of the nest to follow their path, one would expect the ant colony to heavily favour gathering food from the northern pile from then on. This is very different from a behaviour based upon non-influenced random individual behaviour all the way through such an experiment, which, as noted above, would more closely approximate coin tossing. The first half-dozen ants might choose the northern pile, but over an extended period of visits, the colony would be expected to settle down to something approximating a 50:50 split. This emphatically does not happen. The first few decisions radically affect the decisions of those after, and only in situations where the first few make their decisions on something like a 50:50 split does a coin-tossing outcome occur. Indeed, the natural conclusion to draw from all of this is that sooner or later, the system would become pretty rigidly locked into the kind of system that was initiated by the random decisions of the first few ants.

Surprisingly, this conclusion would be wrong as well. Not only was it the case that when a majority of ants did end up visiting one site, this majority was constantly eroded, with some ants shifting to the other site, but on some occasions the proportions between the two sites shifted dramatically, with an 80:20 split becoming a 20:80 split. This apparently perplexing behaviour, as Ormerod suggests, is actually explained quite simply. An ant leaving a nest can do one of three things: visit a food pile it previously visited; be persuaded by a returning ant to visit the other source; or simply decide to try the other pile itself. If we accept the existence of these three alternatives, he argues, then predictability at the individual level goes out of the window, and also at the additive level as well, because the ability to exercise one out of these three possible choices simply prevents the observer from being able to make any reasonable predictions as to future behaviour.

Now human beings may have difficulties believing that ants can make up their own individual minds about which food source to sample on any particular occasion, but it should not be so hard for them to believe it about themselves. Human beings do make choices based upon positive or negative experiences in the past; they are influenced positively and negatively by others' recommendations; and sometimes, just for the novelty of it, they do choose something different, which may then lock them into one choice for a while, facilitate its recommendation to friends, etc. But there is no way of predicting precisely when such choices will occur, or the strength of those choices, or the recommendations when they are made, simply because these choices are made within a much wider nexus of decisions, likes, dislikes, and other events in the individual's life.

All of this argues that much individual human choice, and therefore human behaviour, is essentially unpredictable. Furthermore, human choice is not only additive but synergistic. Like the ripples upon a pond, one person's behaviour and choices will have all kinds of unintended and unpredictable effects upon others, which in turn will have even more unintended and unpredictable effects upon others. The end result is that accumulated human choice is even more unpredictable. Finally, of course, one must place this unpredictability of choice within a universe of even more unpredictable causation. As noted earlier, predictions at the turn of the last century for changes in this one were generally hopelessly wrong. What makes anyone think that predictions at the end of this century for the realities of change in the next will be any better?

Pressures upon predictabilities

Now this is not to argue against the existence of predictabilities. All societies require a degree of predictability and conformity in human behaviour if they are to exist, and the construction and functioning of many of societies' institutions and practices are precisely to facilitate this predictability such that human interaction can take place in a reasonably safe and manageable fashion. Yet a number of things have happened over the last two hundred years to force one seriously to question whether such predictabilities are as certain or as stable as they were, and whether present policies for teaching professions will produce individual professionals capable of dealing with this more uncertain future. A first change which has taken place over the the last two hundred years has been the extensive development and use of bureaucracies, which has greatly enhanced the ability of societies to inculcate and enforce desired behaviours. Now at first sight the development of such a phenomenon – and according to some commentators (e.g. Ritzer 1996), the continued enhancement of such an institution – might lead one to believe that predictability and control were even more certain than previously. There is now, however, a large literature upon this subject (see Bottery 1992) which suggests that an overemphasis upon predictability and control can and does have deleterious consequences upon the individual and the society within which he or she lives, particularly when such bureaucracies attempt to maintain rules and regulations in a world of change which requires very different forms of institutions and practices. As suggested at the end of Chapter 4, this overemphasis upon structured, hierarchical and bureaucratic school structures may be one reason that some teachers behave in maladaptive ways. It is what Merton (1952) described as a trained incapacity to behave in an intelligent (i.e. adaptive) manner, a training that conditions individuals into taking limited and restricted views of organisational functioning, and which fails to locate behaviour within a larger ecological context.

If the desire to enforce greater control and certainty leads only to situations where people are even less well adapted to deal with change, this problem is exacerbated when, as is the case, change is more rapid today than at any time in the past. Whilst the unpredictability of personal choice which Ormerod describes has always been present, such unpredictability is more easily contained when regions, and communities within them, are small, insular and geographically and socially isolated. Social and moral norms were then inculcated in individuals through such institutions as the family, informal systems of education, and the rudimentary penal system, in order that a degree of understanding between, and conformity to these norms, by different members of that community was possible. Before the advent of the nation state, this was the reality to which the average individual would usually have been subjected. They would have generally known little more than their own small geographical area, their local community, the prevailing acceptable mores and behaviours. The lack of any comparison with other communities, other cultures, other sets of values, would have meant that conforming effects upon the individual would have been both effective and profound.

With the advent of the nation state, new problems for inducing acceptable behaviours appeared. The nation state had to replace the loyalty and allegiance to the local community with an allegiance to something larger, more distant, more difficult with which to identify, and used its education system in large part for this purpose. Yet, as argued above, whilst this has been remarkably effective for two centuries, and nation states continue to use education systems in this way, the effects of an increasingly globalised world threaten the utility of this approach.

The argument is simply stated. If a globalised world means that change and unpredictability are the dominating realities with which individuals, communities and nation states have to cope, is it more sensible to institute systems of policy and management in schools that seek to increase control, bureaucratise and generate even more conformist behaviours from its members, or does it make more sense to institute policies and management that create a workforce that is more reflective, adaptable, and – yes – critical, as they attempt to articulate global changes with the values and local conditions within which they work? It will not surprise the reader to find that this book advocates the latter of these strategies. However, rather than simply make this as a statement of fact, it is important to spell out what these major changes and forces are that individuals, schools, communities and nations will have to face. This is for four reasons.

Firstly, because these forces are shaping in the most general sense the way in which societies' norms and values are changing, they in turn shape the norms and values of schools themselves. An ability to comprehend, reflect upon and then sustain or adapt current values in the light of such changes is vital for a proactive response.

Secondly, and following from this, these forces shape the manner in which governments and policy-makers conceptualise the function of education, and therefore the way in which they attempt to direct the work and values of schools, and of professionals within those schools. Comprehension, reflection, and intelligent decision-making in an acceptance, adaptation to, or rejection of such changes are equally vital here.

Thirdly, then, schools need to be aware of these forces in order to debate their power, value and effect. They therefore need to be incorporated as central perspectives in teaching and training agendas, and recognised as major influences on financial and organisational issues of the school, contributing in important ways to the school's 'hidden curriculum'.

Finally, but by no means least, as societies change, so must the work of professionals. Teaching professionals must then incorporate debate on the major changes in their society and a globalised world into debate upon the purpose and direction of their own profession. The following kinds of issues then need to be seen as major contributory factors in the development of an 'ecologically aware' professional.

Pressures of a globalised world

It is important to realise that the forces described alone do not work independently but combine to produce a synergy of change. Thus, whilst the actual number of forces for change that could be described independently is well into double figures, this final chapter will suggest that there are eight ways in particular in which they appear to be combining and impacting, and therefore need to be noted. These eight forces for change are:

1   Most economically advanced countries will have an increasing proportion of their populations in the retired bracket; international economic competition will increase; there will be a continued pressure on welfare-state spending.
2   Most economically developing countries will have an increased proportion of their populations in the younger age bracket.

3   There will be an increased concern over the environment, pollution, and population; the possibility of attempted mass migrations of the have-nots to areas of comparative plenty will loom larger.

4   Whilst the market will not be seen as the best means of societal and economic organisation, it will still be seen as the best means of implementing centrally directed policies.

5   Multi- and transnational companies will continue to expand their scope and power; there will be a continued shift of labour to cheaper countries, and a continued shift in developed countries from heavy to electronic and service industries.

6   There will be continued debate as to whether the influence and power of national governments is declining, or whether they are dispersing functions but retain a still substantial degree of power within their own borders.

7   There will be a continued and increased rate of change in work patterns; there will be a continued and increased reduction in the global workforce at the same time as the population expands.

8   There will be a continued and increased rate of change in society; continued changes in lifestyles and related illnesses; societies will have to choose between policies that move them towards more division or more inclusivity; there will be increased pressures on social stability.

Something needs to be said on each of these.

Most economically advanced countries will have an increasing proportion of their populations in the retired bracket; international economic competition will increase; there will be a continued pressure on welfare-state spending.

A number of writers (e.g. Kennedy 1993, McRae 1994) have indicated a clear trend throughout the developed world; an increasing proportion of populations are aged 65 and over. Moreover, the same trend will probably occur in economies like those of the Asian tigers within the next couple of generations. This has serious implications for the financing of core welfare institutions, for it means that a decreasing number of the population will be paying taxes to keep these going. Not only that, but what they have to pay for may actually increase, because as people get older, so they develop many chronic medical conditions which need expensive remedies. Furthermore, in educational terms, an (elderly) citizenry is created who may be less keen to see money spent on welfare areas traditionally the prerogative of the young, and prefer it spent in areas more beneficial to themselves.

At the same time as these demographic pressures impact on welfare spending, the problem has been compounded for the Western democracies by increased economic competition from Japan and the new Asian tigers of Singapore, Korea and Taiwan, and increasingly from China as well.

Competition will be intense; markets and jobs may be lost, national incomes may decline. It is little wonder that Western economists suggest that one of the reasons that the Asian tigers have done as well as they have is because they spend a considerably smaller proportion of their wealth on welfare, but invest it instead in the economy. Western governments have not been slow to see this, and have largely come to the conclusion that they must take the same road, or, at the very least, only spend extra amounts on welfare if these are produced through greater productivity. Yet not only might such a road pose grave problems for social stability and cohesion if it is pursued; it also fails to recognise the likely reality of the Asian tigers in the next couple of generations. These societies have relied on the institution of the family to absorb the majority of costs of supporting the elderly. Yet as the nature of the job market necessitates increased mobility of a new generation of wage earners, so these individuals will be less capable of supporting their elderly parents, and this responsibility is likely to cause all kinds of social and financial problems within such societies.

The bottom line seems to be this: there will be in many countries a declining tax base from which to fund education and other sectors of welfare. Any political party in power, of whichever political hue, will have much less scope to pursue welfare policies than they have had in the past. Thus, even if, ideologically, they still incline to the ideal of universal welfare provision, they will be very likely to believe that this is no longer a viable option, accepting the reality of no more than an affordable welfare state. Further, with the New Right and public choice writings over the last twenty years, and with Thatcherite or Reaganite policies still held by many in positions of influence, universal welfare provision will not necessarily be seen as a good, some preferring something closer to residual welfare provision. The implications are clear; welfare spending will continue to be curtailed by whatever kind of party is in power. Spending on state education will continue to be squeezed.

However, and paradoxically, education is, and will continue to be seen as, an extremely significant factor in policies designed to enhance economic competitiveness and social stability. The legislation of New Labour in the UK is a strong example of this. Educational managers will then feel three different squeezes: an economic squeeze, as policy-makers try to get even more out of a static or declining budget; an ideological squeeze, as politicians see schools as key areas of promoting social stability in increasingly difficult times; and finally a curricular squeeze, as central government aims to equip a future workforce with the skills it sees as necessary for economic competition in the next millennium. School managements will continue to find themselves being pressured into marching in line with an economic drummer, this time in a post-Fordist uniform, one whose tune is a mixture of the market and central direction.

151

Most economically developing countries will have an increased proportion of their populations in the younger age bracket.

Whilst all this is happening in the developed worlds, the picture in the more underdeveloped regions of the world is very different. Here populations, rather than declining, are expanding at a fairly rapid rate, and this is despite the best efforts of governments to change this. Even though the trend is for family size to decline, as incomes rise and urban populations increase, this is a long-term trend. Kennedy (1993) describes this as like a huge ship trying to stop; it continues to travel a lot further before it finally comes to rest. In the meantime, the problems of population increase continue. Certainly, there has been debate between economists as to whether such expansion is a good or bad thing. Does an expanding population, for instance, mean that there is a larger workforce, and more gifted people to draw upon; or does it mean a greater drain upon resources, greater pressures upon welfare institutions, greater difficulty in simply feeding these extra mouths? The truth probably lies somewhere between. Perhaps the greatest problem, however, is one that, for different reasons, will face the developed world as well – the decline in the availability of jobs. Kennedy (ibid., p. 27) paints a worrying picture:

> ... at present, the labour force in developing countries totals around 1.76 billion, but it will rise to more than 3.1 billion by 2025 – implying a need for 38–40 million jobs every year ...

A lack of jobs, historically speaking, has produced poverty, mental illness, increased crime rates, and social and political instability. A scenario of increasing populations with declining job prospects is not a pleasant one to contemplate. It will be returned to later in the chapter.

There will be an increased concern over the environment, pollution, and population; the possibility of attempted mass migrations of the have-nots to areas of comparative plenty will loom larger.

The environmental implications for the societies and educational systems of the underdeveloped world are frightening; they should be no less alarming for the developed world. Over two hundred years ago, Thomas Malthus predicted that an expanding population would eventually exhaust the food supply as the former expanded geometrically, whilst the latter expanded only arithmetically. He was of course incorrect, failing to appreciate population migrations, agricultural and technological revolutions. Yet the fact remains that there is a core truth to Malthus's argument which makes his predictions seem increasingly plausible: populations in the less developed world are expanding, and because of deforestation, soil erosion, and global food distribution, there is not the food to feed them. Whilst there are developments in biotechnology, which at some stage will probably have a major impact upon food production capacity, there are few signs that this will happen in the immediate future, or in parts of the world required to address these issues, nor is there much sign of wealth and resource distribution from richer to poorer countries. This is leading to increases in illegal immigration to richer countries, and could lead to major migratory movements such as have not been seen for many centuries. The impact on both the developing and developed worlds are difficult to imagine in all its consequences, but it would almost certainly be traumatic.

Furthermore, the global resources of many substances are non-renewable, and the prospect of generating alternatives has not been fully realised. Two or three decades from now, there may be terminal depletion of major global resources, particularly as the speed of their use is accelerated by the continued growth in the world's population, and this poses increasing problems of pollution. The world's nations have been slow to recognise these problems. Yet metaphors for the stewardship of the Earth like that of Boulding (1968), in which he describes modern societies as practising cowboy economics (limitless resources to be used and discarded at will) in a spaceship world (where everything needs to be conserved and recycled, for all depend upon the same life stocks), need to be much more at the forefront of policy-makers' and educators' minds.

Such realisation is increasing, but there is a major hurdle to overcome which few of the developed countries, or their educational systems, seem prepared to confront. It is this. The most obvious way for the two largest nations on the globe, India and China, to improve the conditions of their citizens is to increase their standard of living, to increase their consumption. Yet this will eat up even more of the world's resources, and add even more to its pollution. However, it is extremely questionable whether the developed world has either provided a moral lead in this area, by cutting down on its consumption, or has the right to tell impoverished nations that they should have a standard of living comparable to their own. In Britain, for example, there are 30 cars for every 100 inhabitants, whilst in India there is only one car for every 800 inhabitants. North Americans represent only 6% of the world's population, yet consume 35% of its resources (Ponting 1991). Yet until such inequities are addressed in the developed world, how can the underdeveloped world be expected to listen? And how much of the agenda of an educational institution is devoted to such issues?

Whilst the market will not be seen as the best means of societal and economic organisation, it will still be seen as the best means of implementing centrally directed policies.

Advocates of the market probably had their most triumphalist proponent in 1992 with Francis Fukuyama's *The End of History and the Last Man*, a book written in the early American euphoria at the collapse of Soviet communism. This book, however, has suggested that the influence of the market is still strong but no longer dominating. Post-Fordist views in education elsewhere suggest that governments no longer are attempting to deliver the whole of an education service, or any other welfare service for that matter. It is believed to be far better for government to allow a variety of public and private providers, such that these producers compete between themselves and improve their 'products' in order to retain old customers and attract new ones. Governments can then restrict themselves to setting benchmarks, targets, and quality standards which they can monitor in one form or another. Is this the 'hollowing out' of the state, the end destination being the end of the nation state, or is it rather the 'dispersal' of the functions, the end result being a leaner but more adaptable, and still very dominant state system? Whichever is the case, systems are set up in which schools must compete with one another, making them begin to look more and more like businesses in the private sector.

Schools are then challenged and changed in at least three ways. Firstly, notions of educational communities, and of professionalism as a sharing of expertise, are both dissolved as schools compete with one another, and competitive advantage must be maintained. Secondly, the value of education for its own sake is increasingly marginalised as schools respond to the parochial and short-term wish of the consumer. Lastly, as financial and economic agendas threaten to take precedence over educational ones, so parents cease to be seen as partners, and are treated – and see themselves – as customers.

Clearly, the market cannot be a final or total answer, even at the level of implementation. At the level of the person, the market has a narrow, restricted logic, predicated upon individuals as self-interested consumers which radically mis-describes and limits the capacities of human beings: as carers, as altruists, as dreamers, as builders of a better society. At the level of the state, governments increasingly see its limitations in terms of responding to issues generated by greater globalisation. Finally, at the global level, its effects can be disastrous, for resources are consumed until it ceases to be profitable to extract them, regardless of any future need. Similarly, pollution is seldom taken into account, as its consequences can in many cases be passed on to others to deal with; even where polluters are taxed, the damage has already been done. Thus, unless legislative and ethical frameworks are created that prevent the utilisation of resources simply at the whim of the market, resource competition and pollution will increase such that markets themselves will create conditions in which their own existence will no longer be possible. It is clear that both national and global strategies will be required. Markets may be a significant part of any future jigsaw, but they cannot be the full picture.

Multi- and transnational companies will continue to expand their scope and power; there will be a continued shift of labour to cheaper countries, and a continued shift in developed countries from heavy to electronic and service industries.

It is ironic, then, given national realisations that the functions of markets need to be subordinated to wider societal and state direction, that the end of the second millennium seems to be the age of multi- and transnational corporations. Their power and influence has expanded exponentially. In terms of sheer size, the statistics are impressive. Consider a few facts:

- Five hundred companies control 42% of the world's wealth.
- half of the biggest economies on the globe are now those of corporations.
- Only 27 countries now have a turnover greater than the sales of Shell and Exxon combined.
- General Motors sales revenue ($133 billion per annum) is roughly equal to the GNP of Tanzania, Ethiopia, Nepal, Bangladesh, Zaire, Uganda, Niger, Kenya and Pakistan combined.
- The sales of five Japanese corporations in 1991 were roughly the same as the entire GDP of the former Soviet Union.

(Korten 1995, Morgan 1998)

Further, given that it is a standard economic assumption that a monopoly exists in a market when the top four firms account for more than 40% of sales, it is important to note that, globally, that situation now obtains in significant areas of human activity and consumption. In consumer durables, for examples, the top five firms control nearly 70% of the entire market; in the automobile, airline, aerospace, electronic components, electrical, electronics, and steel industries, the top five firms control more than 50% of the global market; in the oil, personal computer and media industries, the top five firms control more than 40% of sales (Korten 1995).

All this means that multi- and transnationals companies now have enormous clout, a power made all the more imposing by the fact that they are not geographically limited; they can and do shift their investments around the world to harvest the best conditions. Whilst some writers (e.g. Ohmae 1991, 1995) describe this as inevitable, a reality of our economic times, and talk in terms of how to secure one's best advantage within it, others are less sanguine. Korten (1995, p. 126) argues that as localities are penetrated by global firms, it becomes good business for the firm '... to take advantage of the differences between localities with regard to wages, market potential, employment standards, taxes, environmental regulations, local facilities, and human resources'. The end result is one where firms arrange their operations around the world '... to produce products where costs are lowest, sell them where markets are more lucrative, and shift the resulting profits to where tax rates are least burdensome' (ibid.)

One result is what Brecher (1993) calls 'the race to the bottom', where the wages that will be accepted and the social conditions that will be endured fall 'to the level of the most desperate'. And this can result in the kind of advertisement that the Philippine government placed in the business magazine *Fortune*:

> To attract companies like yours ... we have felled mountains, razed jungles, filled swamps, moved rivers, relocated towns ... all to make it easier for you and your business to do business here.

As Handy (1997, p. 77) argues, in the medium to long term, the nation state may try to have some say in the governance of these 'free-roving alternative states'. Yet, in the long term, national governments have been faced with an acute dilemma. Do they, to attract multinational business, engage in policies that eschew minimum wages for workers, abandon legislation designed to protect working conditions, and engineer education systems that provide only a minimum education for a large percentage of the population, in the hope that by making their labour cheap, multinationals will choose them as a base? Or do they accept that the loss of manual labour to cheaper markets is inevitable, and instead engage in an expensive education programme which equips a workforce with flexiblity, adaptiveness, electronic and service skills with which (for the moment) poorer countries cannot compete? It is clear which road the New Labour government in the UK is taking. All the more ironic then, that in the education of its teachers it should be moving in the other direction.

There will be continued debate as to whether the influence and power of national governments is declining, or whether they are dispersing functions but retain a still substantial degree of power within their own borders.

This book has spent some time on this subject already, and it clearly has large implications for schools and education in general. On the debit side, it is clear that there is a drain of power away from national governments. Much of this has been spelt out earlier. Transnational organisations like NAFTA and the EC require the ceding of powers to them from the nation state. The 'hollowed out' state finds itself having to relinquish its commitment to the delivery of services for either economic or ideological reasons. The nation state finds itself increasingly involved in marketing the assets of its country in the attempt to attract transnational investment and more and more of its linguistic and cultural groups find their meaning and identity at a level lower than that of the nation state. The ideology of the market dictates the devolution of responsibility and autonomy to the level of implementation. All of these forces combine to make the nation state less powerful, less influential, both at the level of the functioning of the planet, and at the level of the life of the individual. Forces both large and small are reducing its impact.

On the credit side, however, reports of the actual death of the nation state are still greatly exaggerated. Nation states remain a formidable force, and those in government at this level will do everything in their power to retain that power. This will mean the more conscious and systematic organisation of forces that it can muster. It will mean that whilst in some aspects the state may be hollowed out, it will also attempt to disperse its implementation functions, whilst retaining control of strategy and direction. One clear example of this undoubtedly is and will continue to be the state education system. The paradox here then may be that whilst the power of the nation state may decline in some respects, those employed within education may feel precisely the reverse; that the state actually increases its attempts to control and direct what happens within its orbit of power. If this is the case, it should come as no surprise that those within education feel the moves towards some form of centralisation just as strongly, if not more so, than at any time in the past. And if part of the management of schools is pulled towards the market, competition and customers, another part will be dictated to by governments, either state or national, that see a national education system as one means of shoring up their remaining power, of inducting their future citizens into norms, values, and attitudes suited to their cultural and economic survival. The contradictory pulls of the market and the centre combined into a post-Fordist model will then continue to prove severely disorienting to many working in schools.

There will be a continued and increased rate of change in work patterns; there will be a continued and increased reduction in the global workforce at the same time as the population expands.

The changing pattern of work is visible to all in the Western world. It was only a couple of generations ago that the expectation was for the individual to enter the workforce, and remain in the same job for life. Nowadays, the situation is very different. Not only is there a vastly increased number of women in many workforces, but they are workforces having to cope with changing and increasingly insecure job situations. Not only are occupations overtaken by technology, throwing thousands out of work; individuals are also made increasingly insecure as firms contract out their non-core businesses, and as multinationals relocate their businesses overseas. The result is – euphemistically – the age of the 'portfolio' worker (Handy 1989), in which the change is seen as an individual challenge, but undoubtedly as a good (a change that Handy, in later books (1994, 1997) has increasingly come to question). More soberly, this can result in the creation of what Hutton (1996) called the '40/30/30' society, in which only 40% of the workforce have secure employment, 30% are constantly insecure in the continuing change of jobs, and a final 30% are disadvantaged, unemployed, or inactive. These then have the potential to become an underclass, with all the problems consequent on this, in terms of crime, mental and physical illness, and social deterioration – with all the implications of these for schools and their management.

These kinds of issues have been discussed in considerable detail by Rifkin (1996), who argues that we have entered an age characterised by such increased automation, that the vast majority of individuals cannot expect to have a full-time job – ever. This dramatic move towards automation and computerisation is partly driven by the managerial philosophy of 're-engineering' (Hammer and Champy 1993) – the complete re-thinking of the functions within an organisation, the re-assignment of jobs, and the dramatic reduction of numbers in the workforce through automation and computerisation of work. Such a move has led to the paradoxical – some would say unethical – result of companies with hugely increased profits and dramatically reduced workforces. They pick up the profit, whilst society picks up the casualties.

With re-engineering almost a religion in some business circles, with other companies having to follow suit to be comparable in terms of profit margins, and with no end in sight in the development of automation, Rifkin argues that the reality for much of the Western world is an unpleasant one. At best, more and more people will be chasing more insecure, more low-paid and less rewarding jobs, or, at worse, we face producing societies where more and more people simply chase fewer and fewer jobs. The situation is little better in the less developed world, for technology is supplanting and continues to supplant the work of the peasant farmer, as substitutes for their crops are engineered more cheaply, more efficiently in the factory. This not only throws large numbers of peasant farmers out of work, but in one-crop economies, has huge ramifications for the social stability of the countries involved.

With such a scenario, Rifkin suggests that societies need to reconsider the values it wants its citizens to hold. One of the most fundamental of these is that of the link between self-concept and work. If the situation is either one of more people chasing poorer quality or a declining number of jobs, then if we continue to think of ourselves as 'workers' (albeit most of the time out of work), societies and their attendant institutions will be built upon core values they cannot hope to sustain. Not only will the effects be hugely damaging psychologically – as populations are unable to fulfil expectations they are brought up to believe are central to properly functioning individuals – but socially as well, as massive disparities in income will develop between those few who do have 'proper' work, and the vast majority who do not. Rifkin paints a nightmarish – but some would say not unrealistic – scenario of luxurious walled living areas for the 'haves', patrolled and protected by private security firms, whilst outside lie the vast crime-ridden, squalid areas of the 'have-nots'. If, as happened so often in descriptions of underclasses in the past, the blame for their condition is firmly located with the victim, the outcome is likely to be grim indeed – minimal welfare systems, many living below the poverty line, high prison populations, rising crime rates, damaging stress, and increased mortality rates at all levels of the population.

Now it may all be very well blaming an underclass for not working when there is work to be done, but when most jobs are automated and computerised, or temporary and of poor quality, Rifkin suggests that we have to consider a radical re-working of our conception of the function of societies, legislating in greater job-sharing, reducing the working week, introducing greater wealth re-distribution policies within and between countries, and hugely expanding the importance of the civic and voluntary sectors, such that the individual's self-concept is defined less in terms of 'the worker' and more in terms of the 'civic helper'. He also begins to raise the question of the wider responsibility that business has to society – of whether, in their dealings, and in their treatment of individuals, they should be constrained only by the rules of the market. Rifkin does not provide all or even most of the answers, but he does raise many questions which need to be asked.

There will be a continued and increased rate of change in society; continued changes in lifestyles and related illnesses; societies will have to choose between policies that move them towards more division or more inclusivity; there will be increased pressures on social stability.

One point which has been made in a number of places throughout this book is that the future is essentially unknowable, and most predictions have been wrong, either because they have failed to take some factors into account, because they have failed to appreciate the complexity of interaction between the factors in operation, or simply because they could not know of the existence at some time in the future of an invention that has dramatic effects upon lifestyles. So it is important to point out that the forces for change described above, whilst in themselves strong and important (at least from the perspective of the present), need to be understood as leading to a number of different possible scenarios. However, there is one issue upon which all commentators do seem agreed: the huge, continued and increased rate of change in societies around the world, with a variety of consequences, some inevitable, some treatable, some as yet unknowable. One of the most serious consequences is in terms of health. Toffler, 30 years ago, suggested that the major predictor of illness in an individual was the significant changes that he or she had recently encountered, whether this was in terms of job change, house move, marriage or divorce (1970); and the rates of all these have increased. More recently, Wilkinson (1996) demonstrated that mortality rates are higher for all levels of a population the greater the income differentials that exist within a society, suggesting that building walls to keep out the problems of others within a society benefits no one, not even the rich. This is not just a problem for the developed world. The World Health Organization has published figures to indicate that the world faces an explosion of 'lifestyle illnesses' (*Guardian*, 5 May 1997). These are precisely the diseases of the affluent West: coronary heart disease, cancer, and stroke are now the top three killer diseases throughout the world, undermining assumptions that these were purely diseases of the rich, and that the less economically developed countries were not prey to them. The practices and changes of the Western world, and their results, are rapidly becoming global practices and changes, and are bringing their diseases in their wake.

Conclusion: the teaching profession and the third millennium

The picture painted above suggests that the world of the next millennium will be a very different one from that of today, and will face even more stresses and strains than it does now. In the process, societies, citizens, their schools, and teachers within them, will be severely tested in their ability to cope. How prepared are they?

It will be clear that this book sees the educational system as a crucial institution, and teachers as critical players, in the management of change by societies in the third millennium, and that if societies and citizens are to cope, schools and teachers need to flexible, adaptable, intelligent practitioners. Yet this book has argued that processes have occurred and are still occurring that have led to a teaching force that may be very competent in teaching academic subjects and in caring at an individual level with pupils' problems, but which generally fails to transcend the problems of the classroom. Being truly professional precisely involves the belief that teaching transcends the classroom, and requires of teachers that they take an active interest and have a duty in participating in issues that affect educational, national, and global policies. Initially, this will mean becoming more informed about the forces at work in society and around the globe that are steering education. After that it will mean informing others of such forces, and this will then include a dimension of teachers' work in educating parents and carers as well as pupils. In other words, ultimately the profession of teaching needs to see itself as a profession for citizen education, a citizen education that reaches beyond the nation state. In an age when there seems more and more evidence that citizens are being steered into roles as little more than consumers, a niche more comfortable and manipulable by those in positions of power, where participation is restricted to a vote at a general election, the health of societies may well depend upon forces within them who have the knowledge and the communicative powers to help others.

Teachers need not be alone in this kind of initiative. If, over a hundred years ago, Durkheim saw professionals as the saviour of a value-neutered business-oriented world, the wheel may have turned sufficiently for this kind of role to be taken again. If governments are so focused on the economic, and on the steering of education into being primarily concerned with the provision of human capital, it may take other, more disinterested voices to raise the level of debate as to what constitutes a good society, and of the kind of variety and flourishing that is needed to sustain it. Health professionals could develop further the roles of raising issues regarding healthier lifestyles, and of things that prevent this. Social work professionals could accentuate issues to do with the effects of policy upon different sections of society, whilst the police could take crime prevention further than physical means of deterrence to raise the issue of the causes of crime. In all these cases, professionals are in danger of treading on political toes, and there will be powerful voices lined up against them. Yet if they do not take up the challenge, and provide a dispassionate but informed and potentially critical voice, from where, in what appears to be an increasingly corporatist world, will such debate stem? And if it does not, societies around the globe face the increasing prospect of life choices being evaluated predominantly in terms of economic criteria; of opinion increasingly orchestrated to match current policies; of democracies hardly worth the name; of a global context not proactively but reactively engaged with.

The existence of independent, informed teaching professionals, whose opinions are based on solid evidence and valid research, whose view transcends the school, would be good not only for society but for professionals themselves. They would be in a position to regain some of the respect lost by the public for them over the last few decades. Teachers in particular have much to gain from such change. But whilst their own culture remains predominantly technical rational and implementational, they play into the hands of governments myopically happy to see them remain as such. It is easy for professionals to blame governments for the state they find themselves in, but the truth is stronger medicine. Teachers must look through global eyes if they are to play a critical role in the process of the humanity's adaptation to the challenges of the new millennium.

NOTES

2 CENTRAL DIRECTION, MARKETS, AND THE IN-SERVICE EDUCATION OF TEACHERS

1 These data cover only perceptions of disadvantage, not proof of such disadvantage. As far as we know, there are no comparative data on funding between the sectors which might throw some more objective light on the situation. Having said that, even if there were equal comparative funding between the sectors, this is no proof that such funding would generate an equitable situation. If, as seems clear from the data, the state sector has more INSET concerns derived from imposed legislation, then they may feel (probably justifiably) that they need more INSET funding than their independent counterparts to address these pressing issues. But what, then, would be an adequate and equitable level for such funding? Finally, what one school (in any sector) perceives as adequate for its needs depends very much upon its vision of educational provision, and the level of INSET required to deliver this effectively. This is clearly just as controversial as any of the above. At the end of the day, it has to be to admitted that it is highly difficult to specify adequate criteria for INSET funding that would be nationally and uniformly acceptable across all sectors. This seems to come down to questions about views, values, and perceptions – which is where this note began.

2 A nice example of post-Fordist circumscribed power in education is given by Murgatroyd and Morgan (1993, p. 121) when they give their meaning of Total Quality Management:

> *Basic empowerment begins when the vision and goals have already been set by the school leaders. What a team or an individual is empowered to do is to turn the vision and strategy into reality through achieving those challenging goals set for them by the leadership of the school.* Individuals are being empowered in terms of how they can achieve the goals set, not in terms of what the goals might be (our italics).

7 ACTION RESEARCH AND TEACHER PROFESSIONALISATION

1 A Fordist analysis of society is predicated upon assembly lines, mass production and mass consumption. Industrial relations are corporatist and centred around management and unions: strong central control, with many layers of management to ensure that central directives are carried out. A post-Fordist analysis sees the

information technology explosion as making viable smaller production units, and the same degree of central control with the intermediate layers of supervision. Post-Fordism is then characterised by smaller units, greater devolved responsibility to more flexible individuals, but with the same degree of central control, and with a much reduced central core of workers, many more work part time or on short-term contracts.

2 The others would probably be the splintered unionisaton of teachers' professional organisations, the lack of teachers' time to debate such issues, and deeper conceptual problems to do with the very meaning of 'professionals'. See the special edition of *Journal of Education for Teaching*, vol. 21, no. 1, 1995, on this.

3 See Bottery (1994) Chapter 6 on this.

4 For example, Lewin (1948), and Corey (1953).

5 Such methodological concerns about action research are reviewed, for instance, in Beattie (1989), and Hammersley (1992). However, these criticisms do not seem necessarily fatal to a programme of action research. Thus a concentration on practitioners' meanings and interests by action researchers is not necessarily a major deficiency of method, as long as action research does not limit itself to teachers' meanings, and adopt the belief that 'outsiders' have nothing worth while to offer. Further, the use of a natural inductive approach is no more of an issue than it is for any other procedure, for essentially it is a matter of trade-off between the different advantages of naturalistic, inductive and controlled, deductive approaches, which are well rehearsed in the literature. Moreover, such an approach can be alleviated by a willingness to use the insights of these other more structured and deductive approaches.

REFERENCES AND FURTHER READING

Abbott, A. (1983) 'Professional Ethics', *American Journal of Sociology* 88, 5: 855–85.

Altrichter, H., Posch, P. and Somekh, B. (1993) *Teachers Investigate their Work*, London: Routledge.

Amin, A. (1994) 'Post Fordism: Models, Fantasies and Phantoms in Transition' in A. Amin (ed.) *Post-Fordism: A Reader*, Oxford: Basil Blackwell.

Anderson, J. G. (1968) *Bureaucracy in Education*, Baltimore: Johns Hopkins University Press.

Argyris, C. and Schön, D. (1974) *Theory in Practice: Increasing Professional Effectiveness*, San Francisco: Jossey-Bass.

Armytage, W. H. G. (1970) *Four Hundred Years of English Education*, 2nd edn, Cambridge: Cambridge University Press.

Ashton, D. and Sung, J. (1997) 'Education, Skill Formation, and Economic Development: the Singaporean Approach', in A. H. Halsey, H. Lauder, P. Brown, and A. S. Wells (eds) *Education: Culture, Economy, Society,* Oxford: Oxford University Press.

Auld, R. (1980) 'William Tyndale Junior and Infant School Public Enquiry: A Report to the ILEA', in T. Bush, R. Glatter, J. Goodey and C. Riches (eds) *Approaches to School Management,* London: Harper and Row.

Austin, J. L. (1970) *Philosophical Papers*, Oxford: Oxford University Press.

Ball, S. (1990) *Politics and Policy Making in Education*, London: Routledge.

Baburoglu, O. and Ravn, I. (1992) 'Normative Action Research', *Organisation Studies* 13, 1: 19–34.

Barber, B. (1984) *Strong Democracy*, Berkeley: University of California Press.

—— (1995) *Jihad vs. McWorld,* New York: Ballantine.

Barber, M. (1995) 'Guest Editorial', *Journal of Education for Teaching* 21,1: 51–3.

Barr, I. and McGhie, M. (1995) 'Values in Education: the Importance of the Preposition', *Curriculum* 16, 2: 102–8.

Beattie, C. (1989) 'Action Research: a Practice in Need of Theory?' in G. Milburn, I. Goodson and R. Clark (eds) *Reinterpreting Curriculum Research: Images and Arguments,* Lewes: Falmer.

Berliner, D. and Biddle, B. (1995) *The Manufactured Crisis: Myths, Fraud and the Attack on America's Public Schools*, Reading MA: Addison-Wesley.

Blunkett, D. (1998) Foreword to *The Learning Age*, London: DfEE. Online. Available HTTP: http://www.lifelong learning.co.uk/greenpaper./index.html

Bottery, M. (1992) *The Ethics of Educational Management,* London: Cassell.

—— (1994) *Lessons for Schools? A Comparison of Business and Education Management,* London: Cassell.

—— (1998) *Professionals and Policy,* London: Cassell.

—— and Wright, N. (1996) 'Cooperating in their own Deprofessionalisation? On the Need to Recognise the 'Public' and 'Ecological' Roles of the Teaching Profession', *British Journal of Educational Studies* 44, 1: 82–98

—— and —— (1997) 'Impoverishing a Sense of Professionalism: Who's to Blame?' *Educational Management and Administration* 25, 1: 7–24.

Boulding, K. (1968) 'The Economics of the Coming Spaceship Earth' in H. Jarrett (ed.) *Environmental Quality in a Growing Economy*, Baltimore: Johns Hopkins University Press.

Brecher, J. (1993) 'Global Village or Global Pillage', *The Nation* 6 December, 685–8.

Bridges, D. and McLaughlin, T. (1994) *Education and the Market Place*, London: Falmer.

Brown, P. and Lauder, H. (1997) 'Education, Globalization and Economic Development' in A. H. Halsey, H. Lauder, P. Brown, and A. S. Wells (eds) *Education: Culture, Economy, Society*, Oxford: Oxford University Press.

Burrows, R. and Loader, B. (eds) (1994) *Towards a Post-Fordist Welfare State*, London: Routledge.

Cairns, L. (1992) 'Competency Based Education: Nostradamus' Nostrum', *Journal of Teaching Practice* 12, 1: 1–32.

Caldwell, B.J. and Spinks, J.M (1988) *The Self-Managing School*, London: Falmer.

—— (1998) *Beyond the Self-Managing School*, London: Falmer.

Carnegie Forum on Education and the Economy (1986) *A Nation Prepared. Teachers for the 21st Century: The Report of the Task Force on Teaching as a Profession*. Washington, DC: Carnegie Forum on Education and the Economy.

Carr, E. H. (1982) *What is History?* Pelican: Harmondsworth.

Carr, W. (1995) 'Education and Democracy: Confronting the Postmodernist Challenge', *Journal of Philosophy of Education* 29, 1: 75–91.

Carr, W. and Kemmis, S. (1986) *Becoming Critical*, Lewes: Falmer.

Carr-Saunders, E. M. and Wilson, P. A. (1933) *The Professions*, Oxford: Clarendon

Chitty, C. (1989) *Towards a New Education System: The Victory of the New Right?* London: Falmer.

Chubb, J. and Moe, T. (1990) *Politics, Markets and America's Schools*, Washington DC: Brookings Institute.

Clarke, J. and Newman, J. (1996) *Managerial State,* London: Sage.

Clinton, W. (1986) 'Why We Test Teachers in Arkansas', *Teacher Education Quarterly* 13, 3: 28–30.

—— (1993) Speech 7 September. Online. Available HTTP: http://www.npr.gov/library/speeches/030393.html

Collins, R. (1990) 'Market Closure and the Conflict Theory of the Professions' in M. Burrage and R. Torstendahl (eds) *Professions in Theory and History*, London: Sage.

Corey, S. (1953) *Action Research to Improve School Practice*, New York: Teacher's College, Columbia University.

Cox, B. and Dyson, A. (eds) (1970) *Black Papers Three*, London: Critical Quarterly Society.

Crosby, P. (1979) *Quality is Free,* New York: Mentor Books.

Culyer, A. J. and Posnett, J. (1990) 'Hospital Behaviour and Competition' in A. J. Culyer, A. K. Maynard and J. W. Posnett (eds) *Competition in Health Care*, London: Macmillan.

Deakin, N. (1987) *The Politics of Welfare*, London: Methuen.

Dearden, R. (1981) 'Balance and Coherence: Some Curricular Principles in Recent Reports', *Cambridge Journal of Education* 11, 2: 107–18.

Dearing, R. (1994) *The National Curriculum and its Assessment: Final Report*, London: SCAA.

Dewey J. (1933) *How We Think: A Restatement of the Relation of Reflective Thinking to the Educative Process* (2nd edn), New York: D.C. Heath and Co.

DES (1972) *Teacher Education and Training (the James Report),* London: HMSO.

—— (1983) *Teaching Quality,* Cmnd 8836, London: HMSO.

—— (1984) *Circular 3/84,* London: DES.

—— (1985) *Better Schools,* Cmnd 9469, London: HMSO.

—— (1986) *Circular 6/86,* London: DES.

—— (1987) *The National Curriculum 5–16: A Consultation Document,* London: HMSO.

—— (1989) *Circular 24/89,* London: DES.

DfE (1992) *Circular 9/92,* London: DfE.

DfEE (1997) *Excellence in Schools,* Cm 3681, London: The Stationery Office.

—— (1998) *Circular 4/98 National Standards for Qualified Teacher Status,* London: DfEE.

Dingwall, R. (1994) *Litigation and the Threat to Medicine: Challenging Medicine,* London: Routledge.

Downes, P. (1994) 'Managing the Market' in D. Bridges and T. Mclaughlin (eds) *Education and the Market Place,* London: Falmer.

Downs, A. (1967) *Inside Bureaucracy,* Boston MA: Little, Brown.

Durkheim, E. (1957) *Professional Ethics and Civic Morals,* London: Routledge and Kegan Paul.

Ebbeck, F. N. (1990) *Teacher Education in Australia: Report to the Australian Education Council.* Melbourne: AEC.

Elliott, J. (1989) 'Appraisal of performance or appraisal of persons' in H. Simons and J. Elliott (eds) *Rethinking Appraisal and Assessment,* Milton Keynes: Open University Press.

—— (1993) *Reconstructing Teacher Education,* Lewes: Falmer.

Enthoven, A. (1985) *Reflections on the Management of the National Health Service,* London: Nuffield Provincial Hospitals Trust.

Eraut, M. (1995) 'Schön Shock: A Case for Reframing Reflection in Action?' *Teachers and Teaching: Theory and Practice* 1, 1: 9–22.

Etzioni, A. (1993) *The Spirit of Community,* London: Fontana.

—— (1997) *The New Golden Rule,* London: Profile Books.

Freidson, E. (1984) 'Are Professions Necessary?' in T. Haskell (ed.) *The Authority of Experts: Studies in History and Theory,* Bloomington: Indiana University Press

Friedman, M. (1962) *Capitalism and Freedom,* Chicago: University of Chicago Press.

Fukuyama, F. (1992) *The End of History and the Last Man,* London: Penguin.

Gamble, A. (1988) *The Free Economy and the Strong State,* Basingstoke: Macmillan.

Garratt, B. (1987) *The Learning Organisation and the Need for Directors who Think,* London: Fontana.

—— (1990) *Creating a Learning Organisation: A Guide to Leadership, Learning and Development,* Cambridge: Director Books.

General Teaching Council Trust (1993) *The Initial Training and Education of Teachers,* London: GTC Trust.

George, V. and Miller, S. (1994) *Social Policy Towards 2000,* London: Routledge.

Giddens, A. (1998) *The Third Way,* Cambridge: Polity Press.

Gilbert, N. Burrows, R. and Pollert, A. (eds) (1992) *Fordism and Flexibility,* London: Macmillan.

Ginsburg, N. (1979) *Class, Capital and Social Policy,* London: Macmillan.

Goodman (1976) *Charity Law and Voluntary Organisations: Report of the Goodman Committee,* London: Bedford Square Press.

Grace, G. (1989) 'Education: Commodity or Public Good?' *British Journal of*

Educational Studies 37, 3: 207–21.

—— (1994) 'Education is a Public Good: on the Need to Resist the Domination of Economic Science' in D. Bridges and T. McLaughlin (eds) *Education and the Market Place,* London: Falmer.

—— (1995) *School Leadership,* London: Falmer.

Graham, D. and Clarke, P. (1986) *The New Enlightenment: the Rebirth of Liberalism,* London: Macmillan.

Graham, J. (1996) 'The Teacher Training Agency, Continuing Professional Development Policy and the Definition of Competences for Serving Teachers', *British Journal of In-Service Education* 22, 2: 121–32.

—— (1998) 'From New Right to New Deal: Nationalism, Globalisation and the Regulation of Teacher Professionalism', *Journal of In-service Education* 24, 1: 9–29.

Gray, J. (1992) *The Moral Foundations of Market Institutions,* London: IEA Health & Welfare Unit.

—— (1998) *False Dawn,* London: Granta.

Green, A. (1994) 'Postmodernism and State Education', *Journal of Education Policy* 9, 1: 67–83.

—— (1997) *Education, Globalisation and the Nation State,* London: Macmillan.

Green, D. (1987) *New Right,* Brighton: Wheatsheaf.

Guy Peters, B. (1995) 'The Public Service, the Changing State, and Governance' in B. Guy Peters and Donald J. Savoie (eds) *Governance in a Changing Environment,* Montreal and Kingston: McGill-Queen's University Press.

Habermas, J. (1972) *Knowledge and Human Interests,* London: Heinemann.

Halliday, J. (1995) 'Assessment, Competence and Values', *Curriculum* 16, 2: 130–9.

Hammer, M. and Champy, J. (1993) *Re-engineering the Corporation,* New York: HarperCollins.

Hammersley, M. (1992) *What's Wrong with Ethnography?* London: Routledge.

Handy, C. (1985) *Gods of Management,* London: Pan Books.

—— (1989) *The Age of Unreason,* London: Business Books.

—— (1994) *The Empty Raincoat,* London: Hutchinson.

—— (1995) *Beyond Certainty,* Hutchinson: London.

—— (1997) *The Hungry Spirit,* London: Hutchinson.

Hansard, (1994) House of Lords, Education Bill, 14 March.

Hargreaves, A. (1994) *Changing Teachers, Changing Times,* London: Cassell.

—— and Goodson, I. (1996) 'Teachers' Professional Lives: Aspirations and Actualities' in I. Goodson and A. Hargreaves (eds) *Teachers' Professional Lives,* London: Falmer Press.

Hayek, F. (1944) *The Road to Serfdom,* London: Routledge and Kegan Paul.

—— (1960) *The Constitution of Liberty,* London: Routledge and Kegan Paul.

—— (1973) *Law, Legislation and Liberty Vol. 1,* London: Routledge and Kegan Paul.

Helsby, G. (1996) 'Defining and Developing Professionalism in English Secondary Schools', *Journal of Education for Teaching* 22, 2: 135–48.

Hindess, B. (ed.) (1990) *Reactions to the Right,* London: Routledge.

Hirst, P. and Thompson, G. (1996) *Globalisation in Question,* Cambridge: Polity Press.

Hodgkinson, H. (1957) 'Action Research – A Critique', *Journal of Educational Sociology* 31, 4: 137–53.

Holly, P. (1990) 'Catching the Wave of the Future: Moving Beyond School Effectiveness by Redesigning Schools', *School Organisation* 10, 2 & 3: 195–212.

Hood, C. (1991) 'A Public Management for all Seasons?' *Public Administration,* 69: 3–19.

Hult, M. and Lennung, S. (1980) 'Towards a Definition of Action Research: a Note and

Bibliography', *Journal of Management Studies* 27: 241–50.

Hutton,W. (1996) *The State We're In,* London: Vintage.

Hyland, T. (1990) 'Education, Vocationalism and Competence', *Forum* 33: 18–19.

—— (1993) 'Competence, Knowledge and Education', *Journal of Philosophy of Education* 27, 1: 57–68

Jessup, G. (1995) 'Outcome Based Qualifications and the Implications for Learning' in J. Burke (ed.) *Outcomes Learning and the Curriculum,* London: Falmer.

Johnson, D. (1994) *Research Methods in Educational Management,* University of Leicester: Longman.

Katz, M. B. (1977) 'From Voluntarism to Bureaucracy in American Education' in J. Karabel and A. H. Halsey (eds) *Power and Ideology in Education,* Oxford: Oxford University press.

Kelman, H. C. and Hamilton, V. L. (1989) *Crimes of Obedience,* New Haven CT: Yale University Press.

Kennedy, P. (1993) *Preparing for the Twenty-First Century,* Toronto: Harper-Perennial.

Kilpatrick, W. (1992) *Why Johnny Can't Tell Right From Wrong,* New York: Simon and Schuster.

Korten, D. (1995) *When Corporations Rule the World,* London: Earthscan Publications.

Kuhn, T. (1970) *The Structure of Scientific Revolutions,* Chicago: University of Chicago Press.

Laski, H. (1934) *The State in Theory and Practice,* London: Allen and Unwin.

Lauriala, A. and Syrjala, L. (1995) 'The Influence of Research into Alternative Pedagogies on the Professional Development of Prospective Teachers', *Teachers and Teaching: Theory and Practice* 1, 1: 101–18.

Lawn, M. (1990) 'From Responsibility to Competency: a Next Context for Curriculum Studies in England and Wales', *Journal of Curriculum Studies* 22, 4: 388–92.

—— (1995) 'Restructuring Teaching in the USA and England: Moving Towards the Differentiated, Flexible Teacher', *Journal of Education Policy* 10, 4: 347–60.

LeGrand, J. and Bartlett, W. (1993) *Quasi-markets and Social Policy,* London: Macmillan.

—— and Estrin, S. (1989) *Market Socialism,* Oxford: Clarendon.

Levin, B. and Riffel, J. (1997) *Schools and the Changing World,* London: Falmer.

Lewin, K. (1948) 'Action Research and Minority Problems', *Journal of Social Issues* 2: 34–46.

Lickona, T. (1991) *Educating for Character,* New York: Bantam.

Lyotard, J. F. (1984) *The Post Modern Condition,* Manchester: Manchester University Press.

MacDonald, B. *et al.* (1987) *Police Probationer Training,* London: HMSO.

McIntyre, D., Hagger, H. and Wilkin, M. (1993) (eds) *Mentoring Perspectives on School-based Teacher Education,* London: Kogan Page.

McNamara, D. (1992) 'The Reform of Teacher Education in England and Wales: Teacher Competence: Panacea or Rhetoric?' *Journal of Education for Teaching* 18, 3: 273–87.

McRae, H. (1994) *The World in 2020,* London: HarperCollins.

Marquand, D. (1998) 'The Blair Paradox', *Prospect* May 1998: 19–24.

Masse, M. (1996) 'The Public Service of the Future: Reinventing Itself in a Constantly Changing World', Speech at APEX symposium, 4 June. http://www.tbs-sct.gc.ca./TB/speeche/sp0406e.html

Meacher, M. (1992) *Diffusing Power: The Key to Socialist Revival,* London: Pluto Press.

Merton, R. K. (1952) 'Bureaucratic Structure and Personality' in R.K. Merton, A.P. Gray, B. Hockey, and H.C. Selvin (eds) *Reader in Bureaucracy,* Glencoe IL.: The Free Press.

Moon, R. (1998) *The English Exception? International Perspectives on the Initial Education and Training of Teachers,* UCET Occasional Paper No. 11, London: UCET.

Moore, A. (1996) 'Masking the Fissure: Some Thoughts on Competencies, Reflection and Closure in Initial Teacher Education', *British Journal of Educational Studies* 44, 2: 200–11.

Moore, D. (1990) 'Voice and Choice in Chicago' in W. Clune and J. Wittee (eds) *Choice and Control in American Education 2,* London: Falmer Press.

Morgan, G. (1998) *Images of Organisation* (2nd edn), London: Sage.

MORI (1994) *Public Attitudes to Crime,* London: Readers Digest.

Murgatroyd, S. and Morgan, C. (1993) *Total Quality Management and the School,* Buckingham: Open University Press.

Naisbett, J. and Aburdene, P. (1988) *Mega-Trends 2000,* London: Sidgwick and Jackson.

National Commission for Excellence in Education (1983) *A Nation at Risk,* Washington DC: US Government Printing Office.

National Commission on Education (1993) *Learning to Succeed: a Radical Look at Education Today and a Strategy for the Future,* London: Heinemann.

Neave, G. (1998) 'The Evaluative State Reconsidered', *European Journal of Education,* 33, 3: 265–84.

Niskanen, W.A. (1971) *Bureaucracy: Servant or Master?* London: Institute of Economic Affairs.

Norris, N. (1991) 'The Trouble with Competence', *Cambridge Journal of Education* 21, 3: 331–41.

Ofsted (1993) *The Initial Training of Teachers in Two German Länder: Hessen and Rheinland-Pfalz,* London: HMSO.

—— (1995) *Guidance for the Inspection of Secondary Schools,* London: HMSO.

Ohmae, K. (1991) *The Borderless World,* New York: Harper-Perennial.

—— (1995) *The End of the Nation State,* New York: Free Press.

Oldroyd, D. and Hall, V. (1991) *Managing Staff Development,* London: Paul Chapman Publishing.

Olson, J. (1989) 'The Persistence of Technical Rationality' in G. Milburn, I. Goodson, and R. Clark (eds) *Reinterpreting Curriculum Research: Images and Arguments,* Lewes: Falmer.

Ormerod, P. (1998) *Butterfly Economics,* London: Faber and Faber.

Osborne, D. and Gaebler, E. (1992) *Reinventing Government,* New York: Plume.

O'Shea, T. (1997) 'Innovation versus Control in Teacher Education: the Role of New Technology'. Paper presented to the 1997 SCETT Conference, Dunchurch, Rugby.

Pateman, C. (1970) *Participation and Democratic Theory,* Cambridge: Cambridge University Press.

Pollitt, C. (1992) *Managerialism and the Public Services* (2nd edn), Oxford: Basil Blackwell.

Ponting, C. (1991) *A Green History of the World,* London: Sinclair-Stevenson.

Posch, P. and Somekh, B. (1993) *Teachers Investigate their Work,* London: Routledge.

Prain, V. (1995) 'Competency-based ITT: An Australian Perspective', *Curriculum* 16, 2: 121–30.

Pusey, M. (1976) *Dynamics of Bureaucracy,* Brisbane: John Wiley.

Ranson, S. and Stewart, J. (1989) 'Citizenship and Government: the Challenge for Management in the Public Domain', *Political Studies* 37: 5–24.

Reich, R. (1991) *The Work of Nations,* New York: Alfred A. Knopf.

Ribbins, P. and Marland, M. (1994) *Headship Matters,* London: Longman.

Rifkin, J. (1996) *The End of Work,* New York: Tarcher/Putnam.

Ritzer, G. (1996) *The McDonaldization of Society* (2nd edn), Thousand Oaks: Pine Forge Press.

Sandel, M. (1996) *Democracy's Discontent,* Cambridge MA: Belknap Press.

Saxophone Project (no date) http//www.mhric.org/sax/saxnet.html

Schön, D. (1983) *The Reflective Practitioner,* New York: Basic Books.

—— (1987) *Educating the Reflective Practitioner,* San Francisco: Jossey-Bass.

Senge, P.M. (1990) *The Fifth Discipline: The Art and Practice of the Learning Organisation,* New York: Doubleday.

Sewell, G. and Wilkinson, B. (1992) 'Someone to Watch Over Me: Surveillance, Discipline and the Just-in-time Labour Process', *Sociology* 20, 2: 271–89.

Silberman, C. (1973) *Crisis in the Classroom,* New York: Random House.

Smyth, J. (1993) (ed.) *A Socially Critical View of the 'Self-managing School',* Lewes: Falmer Press.

—— (1995) (ed.) *Critical Discourses on Teacher Development,* London: Cassell.

—— and Shacklock, G. (1998) *Re-Making Teaching,* London: Routledge.

Stenhouse, L. (1975) *Introduction to Curriculum Research and Development,* London: Heinemann.

Tawney, R. H. (1931) *Equality,* London: Unwin.

Taylor, S., Rizvi, F., Lingard, B. and Henry, M. (1997) *Educational Policy and the Politics of Change,* London: Routledge.

Times Educational Supplement, (1998) 'Training Courses Go after Poor Inspections', 30 October, p. 2.

Toffler, A. (1970) *Future Shock,* London: Bodley Head.

—— (1991) *Powershift: Knowledge, Wealth and Violence at the Edge of the 21st Century,* New York: Bantam.

Tomlinson, S. (1995) 'Professional Development and Control: the Role of a General Teaching Council', *Journal of Education for Teaching* 21: 59–68.

Tooley, J. (1994) 'In Defence of Markets in Educational Provision' in D. Bridges and T. McLaughlin (eds) *Education and the Market Place,* London: Falmer.

TTA (1996) 'Final Details of the New Funding and Allocations Methodology for Initial Teacher Training', Letter to Providers, August, London: TTA.

Tullock, G. (1976) *The Vote Motive: An Essay in the Economics of Politics with Applications to the British Economy,* London: Institute of Economic Affairs.

Van Manen, M. (1977) 'Linking Ways of Knowing with Ways of Being Practical', *Curriculum Enquiry* 6, 3: 205–28.

Waters, M. (1995) *Globalisation,* London: Routledge.

West-Burnham, J. (1997) 'Leadership for Learning – Reengineering Mind Sets', *School Leadership and Management* 17, 2: 231–44.

Whitty, G., Power, S. and Halpin, D. (1998) *Devolution and Choice in Education,* Buckingham: Open University Press.

Wilkin, M. (1992) (ed.) *Mentoring in Schools,* London: Kogan Page.

Wilkinson, R. (1996) *Unhealthy Societies: The Afflictions of Inequality,* London: Routledge.

Williamson, C. (1992) *Whose Standards? Consumer and Professional Standards in Health Care,* Buckingham: Open University Press.

Wise, A. F. (1979) *Legislated Learning: The Bureaucratisation of the American Classroom,* Berkeley CA: University of California Press.

Wohlstetter, P., Wenning, R. and Briggs, K. (1995) 'Charter Schools in the United States: the Question of Autonomy', *Educational Policy* 9, 4: 331–58.

Wong, E. D. (1995) 'Challenges Confronting the Researcher/Teacher: Conflicts of Purpose and Conduct', *Educational Researcher* 24, 3: 22–8.

Woods, P. and Jeffrey, B. (1996) *Restructuring Schools, Reconstructing Teachers,* Buckingham: Open University Press.

Wright, N. (1993) 'Counting the Cost of Students in the Classroom', *Education* 182, 9: 156–7.

—— (1994) 'Dear, Dear Dearing', *Curriculum* 15, 2: 57–66.

Wright, N. and Bottery, M. (1996) 'Choice of Inset in the LEA, GM and Independent Sectors: Is a Market at Work?' *British Journal of Inservice Education* 22, 2: 151–73.

—— and —— (1997) 'Perceptions of Professionalism by the Mentors of Student Teachers', *Journal of Education for Teaching* 23, 3: 235–52.

Zeichner, K. and Liston, D. (1987) 'Teaching Students to Reflect', *Harvard Educational Review* 57, 1: 23–48.

INDEX